BILL MANLEY is a lecturer, curator and bestselling author. He taught the Ancient Egyptian and Coptic languages for more than thirty years at the Universities of Glasgow, London and Liverpool. He is Co-Director of Egiptología Complutense and Honorary President of Egyptology Scotland, and works with an Egyptian-Spanish team surveying a pristine archaeological site beside the Valley of the Kings in Egypt. His books include *Egyptian Art* in the World of Art series and *Egyptian Hieroglyphs for Complete Beginners*.

BILL MANLEY

THE OLDEST BOOK IN THE WORLD

PHILOSOPHY IN THE AGE OF THE PYRAMIDS

with 74 illustrations

For Richard Stops, a wise teacher,
& Prof. John R. Harris (1932–2020)
in memoriam

Frontispiece: An Egyptian writer at work, with a papyrus book, reed brushes behind his ear, and a writing case by his knee (see plate VIII). Detail from the decorated tomb-chapel of Ptahhatp II, vizier for Kings Izezi and Wenis. Fifth Dynasty. Saqqara • Page 8: Detail of Ptahhatp's Sixteenth to Eighteenth Teachings, on page nine of Papyrus Prisse • Page 20: Detail from the Rhind Mathematical Papyrus showing how to calculate the areas of triangles and truncated triangles • Page 64: The vizier Ptahhatp shown in his tomb-chapel (see plate XI) • Page 96: Detail of Ptahhatp's Eighth to Eleventh Teachings, on page seven of Papyrus Prisse • Page 140: Detail of Ptahhatp's Twenty-sixth and Twenty-seventh Teachings, on page twelve of Papyrus Prisse • Page 162: The Step Pyramid of King Netjerkhet Djoser (see plate IV)

First published in the United Kingdom in 2023 by
Thames & Hudson Ltd, 181A High Holborn, London WC1V 7QX

First published in the United States of America in 2023 by
Thames & Hudson Inc., 500 Fifth Avenue, New York, New York 10110

This paperback edition published in 2024

The Oldest Book in the World: Philosophy in the Age of the Pyramids
© 2023 Thames & Hudson Ltd, London

Text © 2023 Bill Manley

Designed by P D Burgess

Cover designed by Steve O Connell

The Screwtape Letters by CS Lewis © 1942 CS Lewis Pte Ltd.

Extract on page 141 reprinted with permission.

British Library Cataloguing-in-Publication Data
A catalogue record for this book is available from the British Library

Library of Congress Control Number 2022939808

ISBN 978-0-500-29807-7

Printed in Great Britain by Bell & Bain Ltd, Glasgow

MIX
Paper | Supporting
responsible forestry
FSC® C007785

Be the first to know about our new releases,
exclusive content and author events by visiting
thamesandhudson.com
thamesandhudsonusa.com
thamesandhudson.com.au

CONTENTS

SOCRATES: They say that Thumos told Thoth many things—which would take too long to go through—praising or criticizing each technology. When they reached letters, Thoth said 'King, this is the discovery that will make Egyptians wiser and improve their memories. I have discovered the drug for thinking and wisdom.'

However, he said 'Ingenious Thoth, one person should invent technologies, then another assess whether they are helpful or harmful to their users. Now, you, father of letters—your favouritism has made you describe the effects of them as the opposite of what they are. Actually, this discovery will make the minds of those who learn it careless and not practise thinking for themselves precisely because they put their trust in writing—which comes from outside and the opinions of others—rather than reflecting within themselves and by themselves.

'You have not found a drug for thinking but for quoting. You have provided your students with the appearance of wisdom, not the real thing, because they will have read lots without learning, and they will feel educated when essentially they are ignorant. They will also be tough to put up with because they will end up smug rather than wise.'

PHAEDRUS: O, Socrates, you are too quick to make up stories from Egypt or wherever else you want![1]

PHAEDRUS, sections 274–5, Plato, *c.* 360 BC

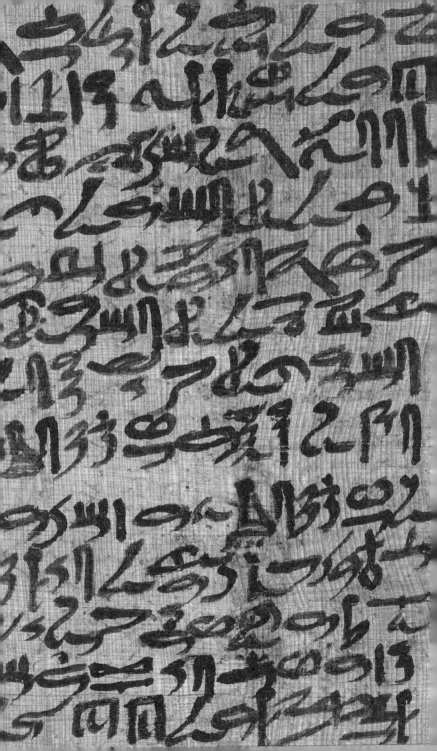

INTRODUCTION

Willingly learn what you do not know
from anyone because such humility lets you share
what each of us is uniquely.
You will be wiser than anyone if you are willing
to learn from everyone.[1]

HUGH OF SAINT-VICTOR (AD 1096–1151),
A Book About Teaching, Book 3/13

Do not be high-minded because you are educated.
Rather, consult with the simple as much as the educated.
The limits of no art can be attained—no artist is equipped
with their fulfilment. Wise words are rarer than malachite
yet found among the girls at the grindstones.

THE TEACHING OF PTAHHATP,
First Teaching

THE TEACHING OF PTAHHATP, written on a scroll discovered in Egypt, was first published as the world's oldest book in Paris in 1858. This was a pioneering era for the study of ancient civilizations, when antiquarians and archaeologists were beginning to scrutinize and control the physical remains of our earliest human history. As such the oldest book might have caused a sensation. Instead, *The Teaching of Ptahhatp* soon gained a reputation as gobbledegook — too difficult to translate, too obscure to read. Sir Alan Gardiner (1879–1963), the greatest modern scholar of the Ancient Egyptian language, described the text as 'quite unintelligible'.[2] Before the end of the century a milestone in the history of us all had effectively disappeared from public consciousness, occasionally mentioned by those in the know but little read by anyone.

Yet, what a remarkable oversight. Surely, in a world now steeped in books and writing, the oldest book would be recognized as one of the crucial moments of human history, comparable to the oldest cave art, Egypt's pyramids or the inventions of the printing press and the internet. Prefacing his translation of the book in 1906, Battiscombe Gunn (1883–1950), Gardiner's assistant and later professor at the University of Oxford, emphasized that the words on this scroll 'stand on the extreme horizon of all that ocean of paper and ink that has become to us as an atmosphere, a fifth element, an essential of life'.[3]

More than simply the oldest book, however, *The Teaching of Ptahhatp* is also the earliest complete statement of philosophy surviving from ancient Egypt and its author even provides us with the Egyptian phrase *merut nefret* that literally translates as 'philo-sophy' ('wanting wisdom' or 'wanting the ideal'). In other words, *The Teaching* is the oldest surviving philosophy book from anywhere in the world. By contrast, the first few recorded scraps of Classical Greek philosophy would not appear for nearly two millennia more. Nonetheless, *The Teaching of Ptahhatp* is philosophy in the fullest sense: neither religious in character nor mythological in form, its commitment to fostering the love of wisdom and answering that perennial puzzle, the meaning of life, is explored as a list of concise, practical insights into the human condition and various conclusions we can reasonably deduce from these insights. Hence *The*

Teaching is also the oldest surviving text committed to knowledge based on the twin pillars of evidence and the awareness of the human mind. The author makes observations about consistent and repeated human behaviour in order to draw conclusions that have 'not failed on this earth in all of time'. Accordingly, he contends, the world and everything in it have both structure and meaning because they have come into being through a creator's intention. In other words, the origin of the laws of mathematics and physics that shape the world is also the origin of authority, justice and truth.

Ptahhatp's teachings are not presented as statutes or commandments but they do aim to guide the reader towards rewarding, productive behaviour and away from futile, self-destructive beliefs. As such *The Teaching* may be favourably compared to other wellsprings of modern civilization, such as Lao-tzu's *Tao Tê Ching*, Plato's *Republic* or Marcus Aurelius' *Meditations*. Like these other, much more recent classics, Ptahhatp's commitment to philosophy is married to a concise, practical writing style as well as an unabashed acknowledgment of the human spiritual condition. Like them also—and despite its reputation among many scholars—*The Teaching of Ptahhatp* turns out to be straightforward to follow, and utterly engaging for a modern reader without the burden of extensive explanatory notes.

The Teaching of Ptahhatp was first written down as a book in the late eighteenth or seventeenth century BC. However, its origin is still more ancient—at the court of King Izezi of the Fifth Dynasty, during the twenty-fifth century BC. This was during the Egyptian Old Kingdom—the seemingly primordial era of the Step Pyramid at Saqqara and the Great Pyramid and Great Sphinx of Giza (plate IV). As such, *The Teaching* as written down was always intended to invoke the authority of antiquity and pass on insights about the human condition that have been true throughout all of our time on earth. The meaning of life, Ptahhatp concludes, is grounded in truth—and truth stands unaffected by time and apart from human intentions. Therefore, his argument follows, *The Teaching* must hold true for any person at any time; but little he says is presented as a law or a proscription. His book is a guide to the human condition based on experiences and observations compiled by the oldest civilization of all. The reader is invited to enhance their personal fulfilment by becoming who they are intended to be or else to commit a 'spiritual offence' — the price of which is measured not in prison time nor condemnation but in futility, loneliness and fear. His only proscriptive statements insist we instinctively recognize human conduct that must always be wrong, such as paedophilia — but not, as has often been repeated, homosexuality, about which Ptahhatp says nothing. Such actions are wrong precisely because they diminish the abuser's relationship to truth without providing any benefit or consolation. In other words, his book is concerned with the quality of our living, not what judgment we may face when we die.

Since *The Teaching of Ptahhatp* was first introduced to a modern audience in 1858, it has become an awkward remnant of the ancient world: difficult but primitive, progressive but hopelessly out of date, liberal but proscriptive. One typical characterization has been that it 'provides guidelines of conduct designed to aid the reader or hearer in getting ahead in life and in being successful, both personally and financially'[4] — in other words, exhibiting the kind of self-interestedness that might arouse the beautiful people of, well, the twenty-first century. If a modern audience, off to work, is embarrassed to read that calculated servility leads to worldly gain, perhaps that is because it is too much like looking in the mirror. A related characterization is that Ptahhatp's supposed wisdom is no more than 'a restorative for the ills of humanity'[5] — a wistful lament for life as it could be, if people were different than they are. Miriam Lichtheim, on the other hand, noted that Ptahhatp's words 'touch upon the most important aspects of human relations' and 'the cardinal virtues are self-control, moderation, kindness, generosity, justice, and truthfulness tempered by discretion.'[6] In fact, for the modern world Ptahhatp's conclusions are stark. The key to earthly fulfilment is absolute self-denial in the company of others: unless obligated to do so by some responsibility or other, refuse to give your opinion, your preference, even your response. What we must seek is not peace and quiet (as in, a lack of noise around us) but a total refusal to contribute to the endless human chatter.[7] It is not the sound of your voice that prevents you from hearing and understanding the world clearly but the incessant static hiss of your opinions.[8]

The final chapter of the present book presents *Why Things Happen*, a sophisticated Egyptian account of meaning as part of the natural physics of the world—again composed many centuries before Aristotle would attempt the same exercise—such that every word, as well as every action, has a definite cause and a particular meaning. In accordance with this metaphysics, Ptahhatp insists that we must practise how to understand the relevance of every individual moment—the 'why' as well as the 'how' of events—by trusting our own mental faculties rather than the comments of others. He provides the earliest—and arguably still the most concise—written statement of the philosophy that this world has a structure made up of certain inherent and unchanging facts, that the unfolding characteristics of reality we know as time and meaning have a purpose, and that we live here and *now* because there is nowhere else to be. In the light of Ptahhatp's philosophy, *Why Things Happen* is evidently a statement of the integrity of physics and metaphysics, and—like the recently reassessed tablet from Iraq, dating to *c.* 1800 BC, that turns out to be full of trigonometry 'well over a millennium before Hipparchus is said to have fathered the subject with his "table of chords"'[9]—is one more instance of how the sophistication of ancient thinking still confounds us, if we persist in looking with prejudiced eyes at our ancestors and assuming they were no more than simple prototypes of ourselves.

Read together, *The Teaching of Ptahhatp* and *Why Things Happen* demonstrate that ancient Egyptian philosophy is not the banal, proscriptive mouthpiece of a despotic regime but rather the reasoned voice of experience—ultimate experience—engaged in an open discussion about the meaning of life and our own place within it. After all is said and done, Ptahhatp says, 'the educated person is the one who nurtures their soul by realizing on earth the ideal self within'. In other words, do not presume to be who you want to be but strive to become the 'You' that is intended—intended for others as well as for yourself—and evolve in the same way that the pip becomes the tree. Such awareness is 'rarer than malachite yet found among the girls at the grindstones'.

In complete contradiction of Ptahhatp's advice, my openly stated intention is that what follows will both establish the place of 'the oldest book in the world' in human history and affirm its relevance to modern lives. We need not agree with *The Teaching of Ptahhatp* but at least we may recognize that philosophy does not have its exclusive origin in classical Greece—that the determination of truth on empirical grounds, and the resolution of physics and metaphysics, were already possible for people in the so-called Stone Age, and that they are witnessed in Africa many centuries before they are attested in Europe. Accordingly, my translation of *The Teaching* in Chapter 3 aims to use plain English in order to be accurate and faithful without being pedantic. Significant differences from previous translations are discussed when they involve genuine difficulties or ambiguities in making sense of the text but, hopefully, have been treated without jargon or undue reliance on Ancient Egyptian words in order to be concise and helpful for the modern reader. The text simply follows that of the sole complete manuscript, which is the scroll we call Papyrus Prisse in the National Library of France. The layout respects the format created by the scribe of the papyrus in using rubrics (phrases written in red ink and reproduced here in bold type) to indicate the beginning of each new teaching and each conclusion. A brief discussion is provided wherever other surviving manuscripts show a significant divergence from the text of Papyrus Prisse or may help us interpret it.

Whether or not this is 'the most difficult Egyptian literary text to translate' (see page 143), my belief—informed by three decades of reading ancient literature in the original languages—is that an accessible presentation of *The Teaching of Ptahhatp* is long overdue. Why? Because we may choose to believe we have moved on from the ancient Egyptians but we need only glance at newspapers and 'rolling' television news regaling us with gossip about power, ambition, celebrity and the dark arts of pretending to be somebody we are not in order to question whether the oldest book in the world has ever gone out of print. The casual assumption is liable to be that *The Teaching* is so intrinsically, irremediably 'ancient Egyptian' that it could have no relevance to the emancipated thinking and lifestyles of the modern world. Of course, this book intends to suggest otherwise, not least by illustrating the sophistication of ancient African thinking and its relentless, resolute relevance to modern anxieties. How salutary to learn that the earliest written witness to the truth of the human condition should have already rejected, on the basis of previous experience, the very essence of modern life.

A note on the translations

The author takes full responsibility for the translations from Ancient Egyptian (Old Egyptian and Middle Egyptian) and other languages in this book, except where otherwise indicated.

In translations from Ancient Egyptian, the sign ... indicates that a word or phrase is missing or illegible in the original text and omitted from the translation as a consequence. The group ... ... indicates an omission longer than a single phrase.

[Square brackets] enclose words that have been restored to the principal manuscript on the authority of other ancient manuscripts.

<Angle brackets> enclose words that have been added to the translation simply by way of suggestion but are nonetheless missing/illegible in the Egyptian text.

In ancient Egyptian writing, the vowels in words are rarely written down, so we are left to read a 'skeleton' word made up only from its consonants. For example, *merut nefret*—the phrase translated above as 'philosophy'—is actually written *mrwt nfrt* in the ancient manuscripts. The absence of vowels is frustrating because it denies us the ability to 'hear' and 'speak' Ancient Egyptian. Therefore, a classroom convention employed to 'speak' the words entails putting a bland 'e' into the skeleton wherever necessary, together with pronouncing the consonants ꜣ (aleph) and W as though they were the vowels A and U respectively. I have followed the same convention here in transcribing Ancient Egyptian words for use in the English text, which is how *mrwt nfrt* becomes *merut nefret*. Nonetheless, as a reader you must appreciate that this convention is a mere convenience and wholly artificial: in reality, we can only speculate as to how *mrwt nfrt* or any other phrase in Ancient Egyptian was actually pronounced.

In this connection, the name of the author of *The Teaching of Ptahhatp* requires some comment. As noted, this is simply written *pthḥtp* without vowels in the Egyptian text and means 'Ptah (*ptḥ*) is satisfied (*ḥtp*)'. Conventionally this has been anglicized as 'Ptahhotep' by analogy with the royal name 'Amenhotep', which in turn means 'Amun is satisfied'. However, 'Amenhotep' is misleading: the 'o' of the element '-hotep' has been adopted by modern authors from the Greek name Amenophis (Ἀμένωφις), which appears in ancient lists of the kings of Egypt. In these lists, Amenophis is undoubtedly used to transcribe 'Amenhotep' but in doing so raises the inevitable difficulty of transcribing names from one language/script into another—akin to the issue of transcribing Beijing/Peking or Bombay/Mumbai in English. Moreover, Amenophis actually arises by conflating two different Egyptian royal names in the Greek lists —'Amenemopet' as well as 'Amenhotep'.[10] Indeed, other Greek forms are also used to transcribe 'Amenhotep', such as Ammenephthis. In short, the Greek form Amenophis is a slender basis for deducing that the Egyptian name 'Amenhotep' was actually pronounced as 'Amenhotep'—still less for supposing that the name *pthḥtp*, which does not even appear in the Greek lists, was pronounced 'Ptahhotep' with an 'o'. In fact, most classical Greek texts and, crucially, much older Akkadian and Assyrian texts more usually transcribe the element '-hotep' in Egyptian names as *-hatp* or *-hatpe*.[11] In other words, the form Ptahhatp has a sounder basis in fact, quite apart from raising the satisfying coincidence that the name is a palindrome.[12]

A note on dating

As you read you must also be aware of the misleading precision of the dates used for the history of Egypt in earliest times. The influential Greek historian Herodotus, writing during the fifth century BC, claimed that the people of Egypt were respected among all nations for having the most detailed records of the past.[13] However, their records did not use an absolute dating system, and instead dated events to a specific year in a given pharaoh's reign (see page 69). Eventually we are able to obtain absolute dates for Egyptian history through synchronisms with other nations, such as Assyria and ancient Rome, which did have absolute dating systems; but the earliest such dates belong to the middle of the first millennium BC, long after most of the lives and times under discussion here.

Accordingly, accounts of pharaonic Egyptian history and culture during the third and the second millennium BC tend to dispense with dates, because they are mostly uncertain, in favour of discussions based on 'Kingdoms' or 'dynasties' or simply the reign of a specific named king. A history of Egypt written by a native priest named Manetho, probably for King Ptolemy II (r. 285–246 BC), established the accepted framework of thirty-one 'dynasties' from the very first king, Narmer, until the conquest of Egypt by Alexander the Great in 332 BC. A 'dynasty' according to Manetho corresponds to a period when one family held the throne in a single line of succession, though he is also clear that occasionally more than one dynasty was ruling at a given time. Consequently, modern historians have conventionally grouped the dynasties into broader eras: defined as the Old, Middle and New Kingdoms and then the Late Period, eras when there was only one king in Egypt; separated by the First, Second and Third 'Intermediate Periods', when the rule of the country was divided, at least at crucial moments. In broad terms we may define the Old Kingdom as the first six dynasties of kings, the Middle Kingdom as the Eleventh to Thirteenth Dynasties, and the New Kingdom as the Eighteenth, Nineteenth and Twentieth Dynasties. Together, these 'Kingdoms' effectively account for the entirety of the third and second millennia BC, but the history of Egypt under the pharaohs had many centuries left to run after the end of the New Kingdom —a matter we delve into briefly in Chapter 5.

The fact that the start of the First Dynasty is conventionally dated about 3000 BC and the start of the Middle Kingdom about 2000 BC seems a suspiciously convenient outcome—which, indeed, it is, because these dates have been obtained by reckoning backwards in broad terms using known reign lengths. A handful of ancient king-lists, such as the Palermo Stone discussed in Chapter 2, do state specific reign lengths and summarize the key events of each king's reign, especially the occurrence of religious festivals, but such lists are too few and often too damaged even when considered together to provide a comprehensive, unambiguous narrative of the kings of Egypt. Nevertheless, within the last decade these broad dates have been systematically compared to scientific models based on radiocarbon dating and results so far suggest that early dates *may* have to be pushed back in time even further, by up to two hundred years.[14] In other words, the ancient books and the people we are talking about here may be even further removed from us in time than is suggested below.

Key moments in our story

3000 BC		earliest kings / earliest writing
	c. 2900	reign of Den (earliest surviving scroll)
		reign of Netjerkhet Djoser (Step Pyramid)
		reign of Snofru (tomb of Metjen)
		reign of Khufu ('Red Sea Scrolls')
2500 BC	*c.* 2480	Ptahshepses as High Priest of Ptah
	c. 2410	reign of Izezi / Ptahhatp I as vizier
	c. 2375	reign of Wenis (Pyramid Texts)
	?	end of Old Kingdom
2000 BC		P.Prisse / P.London 1 written
		Carnarvon Tablet 1 / P.London 2 written
		P.CGT 54014 written
	c. 1070	end of New Kingdom
1000 BC	*c.* 705	reign of Shabaka / *Why Things Happen* copied out
	c. 580	earliest known Greek philosophy
	c. 360	Plato writes *Phaedrus*
	c. 30	last High Priest of Ptah
AD 1	*c.* 50–85	earliest codex (bound book)
	394	last Egyptian hieroglyphic inscription
AD 1000		
	c. 1847	P.Prisse discovered

1

THE CRADLE
OF ARTS
AND SCIENCES

As to those matters which lie very far back,
concerning the lands of several thousand years ago,
it is very generally held that they are the proper
and peculiar province of specialists,
dry-as-dusts, and persons with an irreducible
minimum of human nature.

BATTISCOMBE GUNN,
writing in 1904, aged twenty-one

IN THE NATIONAL Library in Paris are the sixteen handwritten pages of *The Teaching of Ptahhatp*, reputedly the oldest book in the world (plate VI). More specifically, since 1847 the Bibliothèque Nationale has held the only complete manuscript of *The Teaching of Ptahhatp*, which has been copied out in a single scroll along with the end of another book, *The Teaching of Kagemni*.[1] The copy was made late in the period of Egyptian history we call the Middle Kingdom, during the late 1700s or early 1600s BC; and the scroll—now cut into multiple sheets and preserved behind glass in the modern manner—has been known as the Papyrus Prisse (from now on, simply P.Prisse) since it was purchased in the south of Egypt at Luxor, site of the ancient city of Thebes, by the antiquarian Émile Prisse d'Avennes (1807–1879). Reputedly, Prisse d'Avennes procured the scroll from a local man employed to excavate at Dra' Abu al-Naga, an area of hill slopes at the northern end of the vast pharaonic festival site that covers the west bank of the River Nile at Thebes.[2] Dra' Abu al-Naga was being used as a cemetery when P.Prisse was written and remained an area of varied local activity until the eighth century AD, during Egypt's Christian centuries (see page 34).

As early as 1858, the brilliant French linguist François Chabas (1817–1882) had recognized the significance of P.Prisse and published it as 'the oldest book in the world'.[3] Less than a century later, however, while compiling the standard modern edition of the Egyptian text in 1956,[4] the Czech scholar Zbyněk Žába (1917–1971) noted that *The Teaching of Ptahhatp* was already more talked about than read even among professors of Egyptology,[5] though P.Prisse itself remains to this day the 'longest and most perfect Middle Kingdom literary book'.[6] In part, this was because the spirit of the age in the mid-nineteenth century was characterized by modernity, and progress measured in developmental stages from prehistoric to modern. The presumed story of early humanity was re-written to conform to theories of evolution and the three-age system (Stone Age, Bronze Age, Iron Age), adopted as a fundamental convention by the nascent discipline of archaeology, notably through the work of Christian Jürgensen Thomsen (1788–1865). Early *Homo sapiens* (as opposed to other, earlier hominids) was relegated to the

LE PLUS ANCIEN LIVRE DU MONDE.

ÉTUDE

SUR LE PAPYRUS PRISSE.

———

M. Prisse d'Avennes a découvert à Thèbes et donné à la Bibliothèque impériale un papyrus égyptien écrit en caractères hiératiques, qui peut être considéré à bon droit comme le plus ancien livre du monde. Dans son mémoire sur l'inscription du tombeau d'Ahmès, M. de Rougé, dont le nom fait autorité en la matière, s'exprime en ces termes à propos de ce papyrus : « J'en trouve « un exemple dans un document que j'appellerai sans hésitation « le plus ancien manuscrit connu dans le monde entier. Je veux « parler du manuscrit hiératique donné par M. Prisse à la Bibliothè- « que impériale. Rien n'égale la largeur et la beauté de ce manu- « scrit qui provient d'un personnage nommé Ptah-Hotep (1). »

M. S. Birch le mentionne à son tour en passant en revue les monuments écrits que nous a légués l'ancienne Égypte : « C'est, dit ce « savant égyptologue, un code de préceptes moraux dans lequel « sont mentionnés les noms des anciens rois Senefrou et Ani, ou « An, et qui a été écrit par un personnage nommé Ptah-Hotep sous « le règne du roi Assa ou Asseth (2). »

Publié par M. Prisse (3), dès l'année 1847, sous une forme commode pour l'étude, ce manuscrit, si digne d'attirer l'attention des égyptologues, semble être resté à peu près complétement dans l'oubli jusqu'en juillet 1856. A cette époque, M. Heath fit paraître dans la *Revue mensuelle* de Londres, un article intitulé : *Sur un manuscrit du temps du roi phénicien Assa, qui régnait en Égypte avant l'époque*

(1) De Rougé, Mémoire sur l'inscription du tombeau d'Ahmès, p. 76.

(2) S. Birch, An introduction to the study of the egypt. Hieroglyphics, faisant suite à : The Egyptians in the times of the Pharaohs, de J. G. Wilkinson, p. 278.

(3) Fac-simile d'un papyrus égyptien en caract. hiérat. trouvé à Thèbes, donné à la Bibliothèque royale de Paris, et publié par E. Prisse d'Avennes. Paris, 1847.

XV   1

Title page of François Chabas' article announcing 'the oldest book in the world', published in *Revue archéologique* (1858).

brutish 'Caveman', whose benighted kinfolk persisted in the 'Stone Age' cultures of indigenous peoples or 'savages' on 'dark continents' struggling to form simple sentences, still less, sophisticated thoughts. For instance, only a year before P.Prisse reached Europe, the Smithsonian Institution had been established by the United States Congress 'for the increase and diffusion of knowledge among men *per orbem*' — which means 'across the globe', at least to an audience educated in a specific tradition. By 1928 the Smithsonian was able to report that 'the higher civilized man ... may not have the more automatic strength of some primitive people, but his eyes, ears, body, and, above all, the brain are evidently capable of greater conscious exertions, and endure longer'.[7] The Report commented favourably that civilization also manifests in a 'lightening' of the skin, 'a progressive refinement of the physiognomy' and 'more generalized beauty' that 'may now, according to various indications, be slowly proceeding, as in the Eskimo, the civilized American Indian, and the North American Negro'.[8]

Of course, this vain, clumsy characterization of most human beings as relatively stupid, ugly and lazy was primarily intended as a comment on contemporary non-Western peoples rather than peoples of the past. Still, the Smithsonian Report noted that 'Nothing of that nature is evident in old times except in rare individual mental giants. Qualities appear now manifested by multitudes which in the past were barely manifested by individuals.'[9] Half a century earlier, Charles Darwin had made the same point in *The Descent of Man*: 'Nor is the difference slight,' he wrote, 'between a savage who does not use any abstract terms and a Newton or Shakespeare.'[10] This assumption about the human lot actually defines the intellectual environment in which Darwin's ideas first emerged because, of course, he was as much a product of his time as anyone else. As is well known, a theory of natural selection behind the origin of species was formulated at the same time, independently of Darwin, by Alfred Russel Wallace (1823–1913). Indeed, convictions about 'primitives' can be traced along many strands of post-Enlightenment thinking, including the economics of Thomas Malthus (1766–1834) and Karl Marx (1818–1883), the natural histories of Darwin's grandfather, Erasmus Darwin (1731–1802), the music and poetry of the Romantics, and the philosophy of David Hume (1711–1776), for whom accounts of miracles could be dismissed because they 'are observed chiefly to abound among ignorant and barbarous nations'.[11] These prejudiced convictions insist on the naive concept of early societies living in a simpler, more 'natural' state—an assumption that can still lurk in Egyptology to this day.[12] Henceforward the evolutionary 'ascent of Man' would be interpreted as a steady climb to the pinnacle, the modern Western intellectual—you, dear reader.

Accordingly, for practical reasons—perhaps to do with organizing university courses as much as anything—it has since seemed convenient to treat philosophy books as an indigenous invention in the lost works of the earliest Greek philosophers, like Thales (c. 620–550 BC) and Anaximander (c. 610–540 BC). This attitude is epitomized in a tale, widely known in the Middle Ages, whereby logical thought was invented by the Greek philosopher Parmenides (born c. 515 BC), who happened to be sitting on a rock in Egypt at the time.[13] Interestingly, this tale was interpreted by medieval scholars, such as the educationalist Hugh of Saint-Victor (see page 9), to mean that Greek philosophy sat on the bedrock of Egyptian wisdom. Today, of course, the rock represents the lumpen mass of early human thinking and modern Western accounts draw a line—not just in philosophical discourse but in all human history—so that 'with the advent of writing, the belief-driven solutions of the priests began to give way to the logic-based explanations of the first scientists, the philosophers'.[14] As such, the earliest texts from Africa are bound to be primitive, mythological and irrational (or, better still, pre-rational) because the capacity to think, speak and write in modern, logical, emancipated terms was a discovery—a recent discovery made by Europeans whose 'Classical' architecture was being emulated in the political, legal and university buildings of the 'New World', the new 'Republics' and the colonial cities of European empires. By definition, the word 'book' could hardly apply in another part of the world in earlier times, still less in Africa during the Stone Age—the status of P.Prisse as a 'book' became mere word-play. Like the great naturalist George Shaw

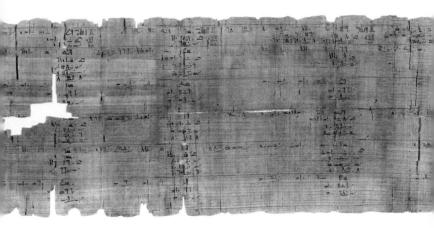

The opening of the Rhind Mathematical Papyrus, which provides a reckoner for doubling fractions with odd numbered units, from ⅓ to ¹⁄₁₀₁. 5.13 m (16 ft 10 in.) long by 32 cm (1 ft ½in.) high. Sixteenth century BC. West Thebes.

(1751–1813) staring in disbelief at a preserved duck-billed platypus on his desk, holding a book of ancient philosophy as a specimen in your hands would hardly be sufficient to make you accept that it existed.

Of course, this attitude is merely dogmatic until we take full account of the evidence, and *The Teaching of Ptahhatp* is among the most important witnesses to the intellectual prowess and humanity of our ancient forbears, perhaps some 250 generations ago. Other than the Bible, for which many beautiful translations exist, the wisdom of the ancient, non-European world is too easily dismissed, the more so since so few people are able to read these books in their original languages—why would anyone bother to learn them? To this day, of course, the physical remains of Egyptian civilization as it developed under the pharaohs are among the unquestioned wonders of the world, as the profound transformational impact of archaeology and tourism on the people and the landscape of Egypt testifies. However, Ptahhatp and his contemporaries in the Old Kingdom, some forty-five centuries ago, did more than

26

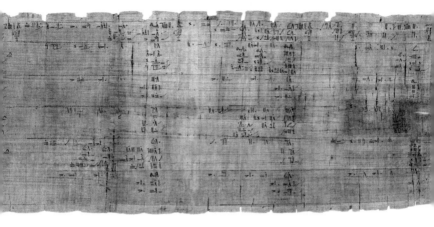

slavishly pile up the stone for pyramids. They practised town planning; organized agriculture on a municipal scale; recorded and costed their activities in written accounts of materials, labour and progress; developed written traditions of government, law and medicine; and purposefully embodied sophisticated mathematics within the spectacular monuments they built to celebrate the meaning of creation. For example, another book, almost as old as P. Prisse — known today as the Rhind Mathematical Papyrus[15] after its Scottish collector, Alexander Henry Rhind (1833–1863) — presents us with eighty-four mathematical problems and proofs, many of which evidently date back to the era of the Great Pyramid, centuries before the copy we actually have was produced (see page 20).[16] To take a single instance of its insights, the formula for calculating the area of any circle as $(d-\frac{1}{9}d)^2$ produces results within 0.6 per cent of our own formula πr^2 but far more simply than using any accurate estimate of π. Perhaps we could usefully teach this in our schools today?[17]

In other words, to read *The Teaching of Ptahhatp* with unprejudiced eyes we would do well to remember that a modern historian's account of the relationship between prehistoric, ancient and modern thought

Athanasius Kircher, German priest and polymath, who wrote the first modern grammar of Coptic (1636) and was the first person to explore Coptic's connection to the 'lost' language of hieroglyphs.

does not have to be predicated upon the notion of inexorable, inescapable progress and increasing intellectual superiority—this is just how we choose to interpret human history today, rightly or wrongly. An older Western tradition, for example, maintained that ancient ideas, classical philosophy, medieval scholasticism and modern humanism are simply 'consecutive links in an unbroken chain' of human understanding.[18] During the fifth century BC Herodotus, the 'father of Western history', traced the very origins of civilization to Egypt. As recently as 400 years ago, the same train of thought was epitomized by the 'extraordinarily erudite works' of Athanasius Kircher (1602–1680),[19] 'the most learned savant of his age',[20] who presupposed that there is 'authentic sacred wisdom in the heathen nations—especially in Egypt, as the cradle of arts and sciences'.[21] In the sense intended by Kircher, we may see the relationship between ancient and modern thought in terms of interesting developments through time, which brought new imaginative horizons to our thinking[22]—but not improvements to our brain, since the physical and genetic changes to our species have been negligible during this 'cosmic blink-of-an-eye'.[23] As such, could there still be lessons for us to learn from our ancestors?

What is the teaching of Ptahhatp?

Formally, *The Teaching of Ptahhatp* is (probably) the oldest surviving and (certainly) the most influential example of a genre of pharaonic literature titled 'Teaching' or 'Instruction' (*sba'yet*) by the ancient Egyptians themselves. The genre has its formal origin in the very earliest Egyptian funerary inscriptions, which became models for presenting yourself to the world after your death, and also offer comments about the final judgment of your conduct in life—comments that rely on truth (*ma'at*) as the basis for justice. This funerary connection with 'Teaching' is not coincidental, as we shall see. Likewise, 'Teaching' insists on testable facts as the rational foundation for knowledge, wisdom and meaning. Particularly in its emphasis on the relationship of meaning to human life, we can recognize 'Teaching' as genuine philosophy. *The Teaching of Kagemni* is a book of the same genre, but sadly the beginning of P.Prisse

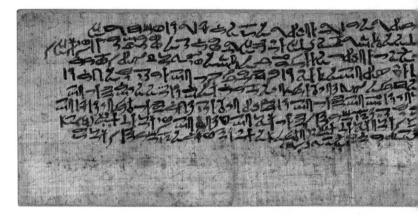

The start of Papyrus Prisse is lost so, actually, these first two pages
are all that remains to us from the end of *The Teaching of Kagemni*.

is lost and with it an indeterminate chunk of *Kagemni*. Nevertheless,
during the last generation scholars have come to recognize more clearly
that ancient Egyptian scribes often compiled volumes of related books
and P.Prisse is a good example of one such volume.

As a specific genre, 'Teaching' is distinguished within early Egyptian
literature because the books typically have named authors (as opposed
to named copyists), which is rarely the case otherwise. A celebration
of writing on the scroll we call Papyrus Chester Beatty 4,[24] dating from
the Nineteenth or Twentieth Dynasty in the thirteenth or twelfth
century BC, urges the reader as follows: 'Be a writer; make it your intention; let it be your identity'. Writing, we are told, is a surer path to being
remembered here on earth than a tomb could ever be:

> Books are more effective than a funerary estate or a chapel in the west.
> They are nearer perfect than temple towers, longer lasting than an
> inscription in a temple.

Then this much later writer names the great early authors of Egypt:

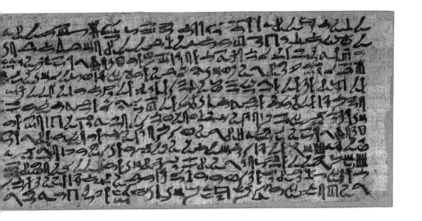

Has there been one here like Hordedef? Is there another like Imhotep?
No one has come to us to compare to Neferty nor Khety, the finest of
them. Need I tell you the names of Ptahemdhuty or Khakheperrasonb?
Is there another like Ptahhatp or Kairsu even?

To the point, 'Teachings' attributed to Hordedef, Neferty, Khety,
Khakheperrasonb and, of course, Ptahhatp survive to this day; so here
we see Ptahhatp celebrated among the finest writers of the world's oldest
and longest-lived civilization. Among his peers, indeed, was no less a
man than Imhotep, reputedly the architect of the iconic Step Pyramid,
who in time came to be worshipped as a god or a saint among fellow
Egyptians because of his earthly achievements (see page 33). Little
surprise, therefore, that Ptahhatp's putative words were still circulating
and being copied more than a thousand years after the man himself had
served King Izezi of the Fifth Dynasty. Indeed, modern scholars have
found his ideas and even his actual words quoted in other texts from the
late Middle Kingdom and the New Kingdom.[25] They may still be quoted
in inscriptions of Tanwatiamuni, who ruled both Egypt and Kush briefly
in 664 BC (see page 174), and even from the reign of Tiberius, who ruled
Egypt as part of the Roman empire from AD 14 to 37.[26]

Wooden box used to store books of accounts. The lid was regularly used as a writing board too, while its length and width are cubit and half-cubit measures respectively. Probably Fourth Dynasty. Gebelein.

What is writing?

P.Prisse has been written by using ink marks on paper to record the words of a language—an exercise which is totally human and entirely without precedent in nature. Which raises another matter: as we shall discuss below, the earliest known collections of ancient books in Egypt are from tombs, including a tomb buried beneath a New Kingdom temple at Thebes and another tomb a short walk away at Deyr al-Bahari, beside Dra' Abu al-Naga. Both collections held copies of *The Teaching of Ptahhatp*. So, before we go on to consider early books, let us be clear what we mean by early writing in Egypt. Though inevitably bound up with language, writing is not a human faculty: it is a technology and, as such, in the human story the invention of writing is more akin to the invention of the internet than to the emergence of language. The real story of writing is not that humanity learned to speak, then write, then use digital media in evolutionary stages; rather, that human beings the

OPPOSITE The deified vizier Imhotep shown reading a book, in a statue inscribed with an offering on behalf of all writers. Basalt. 45.5 cm (1 ft 6 in.) high. Ptolemaic period. Provenance unknown.

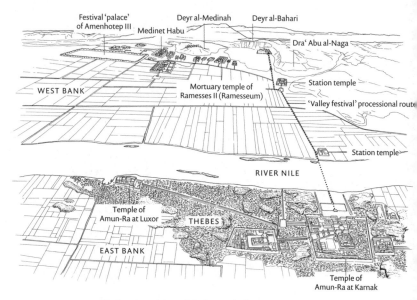

Festival 'palace'
of Amenhotep III
Medinet Habu
Deyr al-Medinah
Deyr al-Bahari
Dra' Abu al-Naga
WEST BANK
Mortuary temple of
Ramesses II (Ramesseum)
Station temple
'Valley festival' processional route
Station temple
RIVER NILE
Temple of
Amun-Ra at Luxor
THEBES
EAST BANK
Temple of
Amun-Ra at Karnak

Modern imagining of Thebes in the late New Kingdom.
P. Prisse was apparently unearthed at Dra' Abu al-Naga, far from the main city,
in a cemetery overlooking the 'Valley festival' route.

world over, at some indeterminate moment long, long ago in prehistory, found ways to express the meaning of things or events in language, music, sports, table manners, burial practices and so on. Much more recently we have found ways to record these meaningful moments in writing, in sound, in images, in electronic data—and these recording devices have themselves turned out to be creative and meaningful media. The written text of *The Teaching of Ptahhatp* is an important early instance of this much more recent technology, and we have no justifiable reason to presume that a book is necessarily primitive simply because the medium used to record it seems primitive to us as we approach the middle of the twenty-first century.

On the other hand, at school in Birkenhead in England I was taught that people began writing by using crude pictures as symbols and only after thousands of years learned how to write sounds efficiently using an alphabet. In fact, presumably as a matter of dogma, I was taught that the alphabet was another Western achievement. A discovery of my time at university was that ancient Egyptian writing is not a kind of symbolic picture-writing; hieroglyphic writing is another way of writing the sounds of words—that is to say, each word is recorded by writing its sound, exactly as I am doing now by writing these words in our alphabet. Of course, we have a cultural bias towards alphabets because they are what we are used to, and we assume that a script like hieroglyphs, which uses hundreds of different signs, must be relatively primitive or somehow constrained by an obstinate tradition that prevented it naturally 'evolving' into something more efficient. On the other hand, if our way of writing is so liberated and efficient, why does 'eight' rhyme with 'ate'? Why does neither word sound as though it has an 'e' in it, when both have a clearly written 'e'? Why do we have no specific letters for the common sounds in 'sure', 'think' or 'that'? Why are there so many different pronunciations of the apparently unpronounceable group '-ough' (enough, plough, though, thought and so on)? How come the way out of this conundrum is not an eggzit?

To colour this picture further, when writing letters, registers, financial accounts or, indeed, literature, the ancient Egyptians wrote using ink and a rush pen in the cursive, joined-up script we call hieratic, a name for the script first adopted under the Roman empire. These cursive documents are usually written in horizontal lines reading from right to left—or, rather, the oldest hieratic documents are written in columns, but the use of horizontal lines was standard long before 2000 BC. This cursive style of writing was used throughout the pharaonic period for anything that pertained to the ordinary business of life, where elaborate, decorative hieroglyphs would be an unnecessary complication for the writer, rather than a welcome adornment. In effect, the relationship is the same as that between modern sign-writing (hieroglyphs), which is designed to be both decorative and legible, and your own individual handwriting (hieratic), which is only as decorative and legible as you can manage.

Wadi al-Jarf Papyrus A, the logbook of a boat transporting limestone across the River Nile to the construction site of the Great Pyramid at Giza. 19.5 cm (7½ in.) high. Fourth Dynasty.

Perhaps you will object that, at the very beginning of history, human beings were certainly more primitive than we are today, so writing must have been symbolic picture-writing to begin with and only became more sophisticated through time. However, in Egypt at least, there is little (arguably, no) evidence to support this assumption. For one, there is no apparent period of 'primitive' writing in Egypt, when pictures were used as symbols to write crude messages. Moreover, taking into account the vagaries of what is liable to survive in the archaeological record, the use of cursive writing on perishable materials seems to be effectively as old as the oldest hieroglyphic inscriptions on monuments. For example, the oldest surviving scrolls, albeit unused and blank, were found in the tomb of Hmaka, a high official for Den, a king of the First Dynasty. At least one of these scrolls was smoothed to create a fine writing surface, and interred in a decorated wooden box.[27] Hmaka's tomb was hugely impressive—covered by a rectangular tumulus or mastaba nearly 60 metres (200 feet) in length, with a monumental staircase descending below the ground to the burial chamber—and indicates an intimate relationship from the start between writing and authority on the one hand, and writing and scrolls on the other. Actual hieratic writing has been found on pots buried beneath the Step Pyramid and on storage jars from Elephantine in the far south of the country, both dating to the Third Dynasty.[28] Then, in 2013, excavations at an ancient harbour on the Red Sea uncovered the logbooks and papers of an official named Merer, who once led a team delivering fine limestone to the construction site of the Great Pyramid at Giza during the Fourth Dynasty.[29] A wooden box with pens and twelve books of estate-management accounts, including the record of a house sale, found in an anonymous tomb at Gebelein in the south of Egypt, also dates from the Fourth Dynasty or perhaps a little later (see page 32).[30] To be clear, all this writing activity predates our Ptahhatp by many decades—and dates from a time when high officials and royal sons especially were occasionally represented as scribes in funerary art, as we shall discuss in Chapter 2.

In fact, the earliest Egyptian texts use exactly the same writing principles as those thousands of years later and 'there can be no doubt that

Label from a First Dynasty king's tomb. Like all later hieroglyphic texts, his name and the rest of the inscription are written phonetically by rebus. Ivory. 5 cm (2 in.) wide. First Dynasty, reign of Den. Abydos.

at least from the [prehistoric] Naqada IIIA2 period (3250 BC) onward, hieroglyphic signs stood for certain phonetic values'.[31] They do so by means of a sophisticated rebus, which is the way of writing that involves using pictures to write sounds, in the same way that we could choose to write the English word 'pennies' as ✐ ∫ ∫ 'pen-knees' or 'guise' as 🏠 👁 👁 'guy-eyes'. Of course, the word 'pennies' has nothing to do with 'pens' or 'knees' but different words in a given language may just happen to sound the same. On the other hand, you could properly insist that ✐ ∫ ∫ more likely reads 'right feet' ('write-feet'), so a rebus is a clumsy, ineffective way of writing unless we have all already agreed which signs to use and how to read them—which in turn emphasizes that writing in Egypt came about through a moment of invention rather than an unprompted, protracted process of development. There were, in fact, several instances of the writing system in Egypt being thoroughly revised, including the invention of writing (First Dynasty or before); the shift from columns to horizontal lines when writing documents (Sixth Dynasty?); rearranging the layout of hieroglyphs in monumental inscriptions (Nineteenth Dynasty); revising the cursive script used for new administrative documents (seventh century BC); and revising the forms of individual hieroglyphs in inscriptions (second century BC). Each instance suggests that members of the palace community had both the awareness and the authority to adjust the scripts but never did change their basic principles of writing, even when they became acquainted with alphabets maybe 3,000 years ago. Whatever the case, lengthy inscriptions first appear in the tombs of royal officials of the Third and Fourth Dynasties, where they are written using the same hieroglyphic script still employed in Egypt under the Roman empire. Arguably the earliest of these inscriptions recounts the remarkable career of a man named Metjen, which we will return to in Chapter 2.

What is a book?

If writing is a technology devised at a particular moment in time, in the case of Egypt, then what could we mean by the phrase 'the oldest book in the world'? First of all, we cannot simply understand a book as a collection of pages bound together in a stiff cover. In formal terms what we usually call a book is actually a codex, and the last generation of scholarship has determined that a codex of paper sheets bound along a spine to form a book is actually the work of early Christians in propagating *ta Bublia*, the Bible. Indeed, there is ongoing debate about whether the codex format existed at all prior to its adoption by Christians, but there is no doubting 'the phenomenon that early Christianity adopted the codex and in time this led to its popularisation'[32]—in this regard, Professor Sean Adams, a colleague at the University of Glasgow, memorably described the early Christians to me as 'iPhone people'—and Egypt is one of the first countries in which we see this new device widely used. Of course, the upshot is that we should not expect to find anything that formally resembles a bound book much earlier than the advent of Christianity in Egypt.

In Mesopotamia, texts of many kinds had long since been written instead on mud tablets, often shaped and sized to fit the palm of a scribe's hand and later baked hard for storage. Such tablets could be

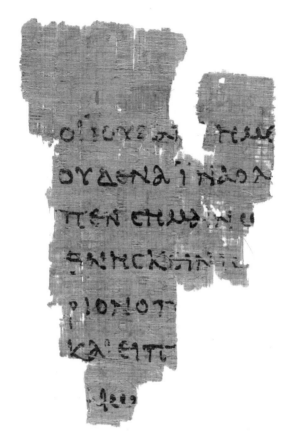

ABOVE Possibly the oldest surviving fragment of a Christian book,
verses from John's Gospel found in Egypt. Papyrus. 9 cm (3½ in.) high.
Early second century AD. Oxyrhynchus.
OVERLEAF An early Greek edition of Paul's Epistles exhibits
the familiar codex format of a modern book, with numbered pages
folded and bound along the spine. Papyrus. 19 cm (7½ in.) high.
Third century AD. Purchased in Egypt.

ΠΟ ΡΑ ΦΥΣΙΝ ΕΝΕΚΕΝΤΡΙΣΘΗϹ ΕΙϹ ΚΑΛΛΙ
ΕΛΑΙΟΝ ΠΟϹΩ ΜΑΛΛΟΝ ΟΥΤΟΙ ΚΑΤΑ ΦΥϹΙΝ
ΕΝΚΕΝΤΡΙϹΘΗϹΟΝΤΑΙ ΤΗΙ ΔΙΑ ΕΛΕΑ ΟΥ
ΓΑΡ ΘΕΛΩ ΥΜΑϹ ΑΓΝΟΕΙΝ ΑΔΕΛΦΟΙ ΤΟ ΜΥ
ϹΤΗΡΙΟΝ ΤΟΥΤΟ ΙΝΑ ΜΗ ΗΤΕ ΕΑΥΤΟΙϹ ΦΡΟ
ΝΙΜΟΙ ΟΤΙ ΠΟΡΩϹΙϹ ΑΠΟ ΜΕΡΟΥϹ ΤΩΙ ΙϹΡΑΗΛ
ΓΕΓΟΝΕΝ ΑΧΡΙ ΟΥ ΤΟ ΠΛΗΡΩΜΑ ΤΩΝ ΕΘΝΩΝ
ΕΙϹ ΕΛΘΗ ΚΑΙ ΟΥΤΩϹ ΠΑϹ ΙϹΡΑΗΛ ϹΩΘΗϹΕΤ
ΚΑΘΩϹ ΓΕΓΡΑΠΤΑΙ ΗΞΕΙ ΕΚ ϹΕΙΩΝ Ο ΡΥΟ
ΜΕΝΟϹ ΑΠΟϹΤΡΕΨΕΙ ΑϹΕΒΕΙϹ ΑΠΟ ΙΑΚΩΒ
ΚΑΙ ΑΥΤΗ ΑΥΤΟΙϹ ΠΑΡ ΕΜΟΥ Η ΔΙΑΘΗΚΗ
ΟΤΑΝ ΑΦΕΛΩΜΑΙ ΤΑϹ ΑΜΑΡΤΙΑϹ ΑΥΤΩΝ
ΚΑΤΑ ΜΕΝ ΤΟ ΕΥΑΓΓΕΛΙΟΝ ΕΧΘΡΟΙ ΔΙ ΥΜ
ΑϹ ΔΕ ΤΗΝ ΕΚΛΟΓΗΝ ΑΓΑΠΗΤΟΙ ΔΙΑ
ΤΟΥϹ ΠΑΤΕΡΑϹ ΑΜΕΤΑΜΕΛΗΤΑ ΓΑΡ ΤΑ ΧΑΡΙϹ
ΜΑΤΑ ΚΑΙ Η ΚΛΗϹΙϹ ΤΟΥ ΘΥ ΩϹΠΕΡ ΓΑΡ ΥΜΕ
ΙϹ Η ΠΕΙΘΗϹΑΤΕ ΤΩ ΘΩ ΝΥΝ ΔΕ ΗΛΕΗ
ΘΗ ΤΕ ΤΗ ΤΟΥΤΩΝ ΑΠΙΘΕΙΑ ΟΥΤΩϹ ΚΑΙ ΟΥ
ΤΟΙ ΝΥΝ Η ΠΕΙΘΗϹΑΝ ΤΩ ΥΜΕΤΕΡΩ ΕΛΕΕΙ ΙΝ
ΚΑΙ ΑΥΤΟΙ ΕΛΕΗΘΩϹΙΝ ϹΥΝΕΚΛΕΙϹΕΝ ΓΑ
Ο ΘϹ ΤΟΥϹ ΠΑΝΤΑϹ ΕΙϹ ΑΠΙΘΕΙΑΝ ΙΝΑ ΤΟΥϹ ΠΑ

ΑΝΤΕCΜΟΥΤΗΟΛΙΨΕΙ ΟΥΔΑΛΛΑ ΚΑ[
ΙΟΙ ΟΤΙ ΕΝ ΑΡΧΗ ΤΟΥ ΕΥΑΓΓΕΛΙΟΥ ΟΤΕ ΕΞΗΛΘΟ[
ΠΟ ΜΑΚΕΔΟΝΙΑC ΟΥΔΕΜΙΑ ΜΟΙ ΕΚΚΛΗCΙΑ ΕΚΟΙ[
ΙΗCΕΝ ΕΙC ΛΟΓΟΝ ΔΟCΕΩC ΚΑΙ ΛΗΜΨΕΩC ΕΙ ΜΗ ΥΜΕ[
ΛΟΜΟΝ ΟΤΙ ΚΑΙ ΕΝ ΘΕCCΑΛΟΝΕΙΚΗ ΚΑΙ ΑΠΑΞ ΚΑΙ
ΕΙC ΤΗΝ ΧΡΕΙΑΝ ΜΟΙ ΕΠΕΜΨΑΤΕ ΟΥΧ ΟΤΙ ΕΠΙΖΗΤ[
ΤΟ ΔΟΜΑ ΑΛΛΑ ΕΠΙΖΗΤΩ ΤΟΝ ΚΑΡΠΟΝ ΤΟΝ ΠΛΕΟΝΑΖΟΝΤΑ ΕΙC ΛΟΓΟΝ ΥΜΩ[
ΑΠΕΧΩ ΔΕ ΠΑΝΤΑ ΚΑΙ ΠΕΡΙCCΕΥΩ ΠΕΠΛΗΡΩΜΑΙ
ΔΕΞΑΜΕΝΟC ΠΑΡΑ ΕΠΑΦΡΟΔΕΙΤΟΥ ΤΑ ΠΑΡ
ΥΜΩΝ ΟCΜΗΝ ΕΥΩΔΙΑC ΘΥCΙΑΝ ΔΕΚΤΗΝ ΕΥΑΡΕ
CΤΟΝ ΤΩ ΘΩ Ο ΔΕ ΘΕΟC ΜΟΥ ΠΛΗΡΩCΕΙ ΠΑCΑΝ ΧΡΕΙΑ[
ΥΜΩΝ ΚΑΤΑ ΤΟ ΠΛΟΥΤΟC ΑΥΤΟΥ ΕΝ ΔΟΞΗ ΕΝ ΧΡΩ
ΙΗΥ ΤΩ ΔΕ ΘΩ ΚΑΙ ΠΡΙ ΗΜΩΝ Η ΔΟΞΑ ΕΙC ΤΟΥC ΑΙΩ
ΝΑC ΤΩΝ ΑΙΩΝΩΝ ΑΜΗΝ ΑCΠΑCΑCΘΕ ΠΑΝΤΑ
ΑΓΙΟΝ ΕΝ ΧΩ ΙΗΥ ΑCΠΑΖΟΝΤΑΙ ΥΜΑC ΟΙ CΥΝ
ΕΜΟΙ ΑΔΕΛΦΟΙ ΑCΠΑΖΟΝΤΑΙ ΥΜΑC ΠΑΝΤΕC ΟΙ Α
ΜΑΛΙCΤΑ ΔΕ ΟΙ ΕΚ ΤΗC ΚΑΙCΑΡΟC ΟΙΚΙΑC Η Χ[
ΤΟΥ ΚΥ ΗΜΩΝ ΙΗΥ ΧΡΥ ΜΕΤΑ ΤΟΥ ΠΝC ΥΜΩ[
ΑΜΗΝ

ΠΡΟC ΚΟΛΑCCΑΕΙC

ΠΑΥΛΟC ΑΠΟCΤΟΛΟC ΧΡΥ ΙΗΥ ΔΙΑ ΘΕ[
ΘΥ ΚΑΙ ΤΕΜΟΘΕΟC Ο ΑΔΕΛΦΟ[

boxed together to create collections in the manner of the thousands of tablets found in the famous palace library of King Assurbanipal (r. *c.* 669–630 BC) at Nineveh in Assyria, or the remarkable archive of more than 350 letters found at an Eighteenth Dynasty government office in Middle Egypt, mostly written in Babylonian, a language from ancient Iraq.[33] This might even have been the format in which some of the earliest books of the Bible were originally written down too,[34] but in their present forms, like Assurbanipal's library, they certainly postdate the writing of P.Prisse by many, many centuries. The same holds true for the dates of the earliest books from India and Pakistan, and even the earliest writing in China, Europe or America.

Along the Egyptian Nile, by contrast, through 3,000 years of pharaonic civilization—and several centuries more under Roman rule—the typical writing medium for cursive texts was the ostracon, which is no more than a limestone flake or a ceramic sherd, selected for use on the basis of a convenient size and shape (see page 137). Ostraca, being no more than bits of broken pottery or stones from the ground, were first and foremost readily available—but they were also durable, erasable and not at all prone to blowing away in the prevailing wind along the Nile Valley.[35] From the New Kingdom onwards, hieratic copies of texts were sometimes also written on plastered writing boards, which were in effect artificial ostraca, equally well suited to reuse, to archiving and to storage (see page 51). However, a 'book' of any significant length would entail using either multiple ostraca, which could be boxed up but not easily bound together, or a single large and potentially cumbersome ostracon. Consequently, a more appropriate medium for compiling books was papyrus—a tough, flexible paper that can easily be cut to size, and just as easily glued to other sheets to create the familiar roll or scroll (see frontispiece). If we had access to the original, iconic Library of Alexandria, most of the books we would find there would be scrolls of this kind, and papyrus was used in Egypt for writing until the tenth century AD.[36] Accordingly, a rolled-up scroll is basically how books were understood in the classical world—'when the ancient Greeks thought of a book they had a papyrus roll in mind.'[37] Many of our own words for books and writing come from words in Greek

A most portable book format, the rolled papyrus scroll.
This example weighs 350 grams (12 oz.), and its circumference
(about 20 cm or 8 in.) easily fits a typical adult hand span.

(bibliophile, tome, encyclopaedia, synopsis) or Latin (pen, volume, library, letter), whereas in the Ancient Egyptian language a book written in a scroll was a *mejaat*, or later *joome*.

Papyrus itself is a very tall, essentially African plant, which used to grow widely in the near-stagnant marshes of Egypt, especially in the Nile Delta. Its Ancient Egyptian name was *tjuwf*, so the origin of the Greek word *papyrus* is a matter for speculation—though obviously in turn it is the basis of our own word 'paper'. Papyrus stems were harvested in lengths convenient for carrying, then peeled, sliced and laid in fine strips across a board (plate 1). Another fine layer of strips would be laid at right angles to the first, and the whole arrangement pressed or hammered until the battered pith naturally glued the strips together as a pliable sheet or *qa'hit*, as fine as a tenth of a millimetre. In the case of P.Prisse the width of each sheet varies considerably, from 12 to 41 centimetres (4¾ to 16⅛ inches). After its surface had been smoothed with a stone, a sheet would be nearly white—despite the dramatic 'browning' that often mars ancient paper in modern times— and could be folded or, more naturally, rolled with the vertical strips on the outside so they do not come apart in the process.

At the time P.Prisse was written, sheets of papyrus were typically manufactured with a height of about 30 centimetres (12 inches), which is roughly the height of British A4 paper or slightly taller than US Letter. Accordingly, then as now, a full-size sheet was well suited for texts that use columns of information, such as financial calculations. Alternatively, a full-size sheet could be folded in half and cut with a knife, then folded and cut again, to produce four sheets each of the typical size for an ancient letter. Usually, however, papyrus left the factory not as individual sheets but as a scroll, or *shefdu* in Ancient Egyptian, of twenty sheets glued together (see page 135). The first thing a scribe would often do on taking delivery of the new scroll would be to slice it across the middle and create a pair of scrolls each about 15 centimetres (6 inches) high, which is accordingly the height of P.Prisse. As such, the scroll, when rolled into a cylinder and set down flat, would not look totally out of place on a modern bookshelf, where it would sit about as deep as a typical paperback novel. Incidentally, P.Prisse as discovered has nineteen pages, which suggests it is essentially one complete scroll, though we still cannot be sure how many pages are missing from the beginning because the scribe would readily paste on extra pages at the end as and when necessary.

To write a book, the scribe would sit on the floor with the scroll in his left hand and roll it out with his right hand to form a blank page across his lap (plate IX). Accordingly, the first page of an ancient Egyptian book is on the far right, and the width of each page was no greater than the width of the scribe's lap, typically about 40 centimetres (15¾ inches),[38] though in P.Prisse the pages vary considerably from 17 to 59 centimetres (6¾ to 23¼ inches) wide. Because the vertical strips were naturally on the outside of a rolled-up scroll, the side with horizontal strips would be the first side to write on, referred to in scholarship as the recto (front). The scribe would then start writing from the top right-hand corner (plate VIII). P.Prisse has twelve, thirteen or fourteen cursive lines on each full page,[39] and the scribe wrote five or six signs with each dip of a pen in the black or red ink, according to the close examination made by Gustave Jéquier (1868–1946) for the original facsimile publication of the principal manuscripts of *The Teaching of Ptahhatp*.[40]

Once a page was full, the scribe would pull it off his lap with his right hand and let it fall to the floor, thereby unrolling across his lap the adjacent blank area, i.e. the next page. Once the recto was filled, the scribe could either turn the scroll over and continue writing on the back—referred to as the verso (back) in scholarship—or else paste on extra sheets. Completed books, as they have been found in tombs, were typically stored in a labelled wooden box or a plain ceramic jar,[41] but while in use would be much more portable than you may suppose (see page 45). For example, the Egyptologist Ludwig Borchardt (1863–1938) calculated that one particular scroll, which is 4.71 metres (15½ feet) long, as discovered had been rolled into a cylinder with a circumference of just 16 centimetres (6¼ inches). In ordinary use, it seems a scroll might not have become too awkward to roll up and grip in the hand until it stretched beyond 10 metres (33 feet) in length.[42] That said, a voluminous official summary of endowments of land and labour made to various new temples during the reign of Ramesses III is written on a scroll more than 42 metres (138 feet) long, purchased at Luxor in 1855.[43] A reader, of course, held the book in the same manner as its scribe, unrolling one page at a time, letting it fall to the floor as each new page was unrolled.

Taking stock of our manuscripts[44]

Following Jéquier's facsimile publication of the hieratic manuscripts in 1911, another Swiss scholar, Eugène Dévaud (1878–1929), published the first scholarly transcription of *The Teaching of Ptahhatp* in 1916.[45] As was not uncommon during the twentieth century, this exercise effectively removed the text from general circulation and put it into the hands of a single expert, while said expert prepared the 'definitive' commentary. As early as 1917 Gardiner was lamenting that 'it is far more desirable for our science that he should publish his results without delay than that he should withhold them in view of a perfection that is unattainable'.[46] In the event, his plea went unanswered before Dévaud's untimely death and the obligation was not met until the 1956 transcription and commentary by Žába, based on his doctoral thesis at Charles University

LE PAPYRUS PRISSE

ET SES VARIANTES

PAPYRUS DE LA BIBLIOTHÈQUE NATIONALE (N⁰ˢ 183 à 194)

PAPYRUS 10371 ET 10435 DU BRITISH MUSEUM

TABLETTE CARNARVON AU MUSÉE DU CAIRE

PUBLIÉS EN FAC-SIMILÉ
(16 PLANCHES EN PHOTOTYPIE)

AVEC INTRODUCTION

PAR

G. JÉQUIER

PARIS
LIBRAIRIE PAUL GEUTHNER
68, RUE MAZARINE (VIᵉ)
—
1911

Title page of Gustave Jéquier's 1911 book, bringing together
all the copies, then known, of *The Teaching of Ptahhatp*.

in Prague. Notably, whereas Dévaud freely altered the text to 'correct' supposed mistakes in the original Egyptian, Žába supposed that the number of errors was minimal and made only 'two or three' changes.[47] Although it has been supplemented by some 'extremely threadbare fragments' since,[48] Žába's edition of *The Teaching of Ptahhatp* remains indispensable to this day,[49] and is based not just on P.Prisse but on most of the surviving manuscripts, which are as follows.

Papyrus Prisse

First and foremost, of course, there is P.Prisse itself which, as discovered, measured slightly over 7 metres (23 feet 7 inches) when fully unrolled. As we have noted, it has nineteen pages, in extremely good condition after nearly 4,000 years, but the beginning of the scroll is missing. The first two pages give the end of *The Teaching of Kagemni*, while the third is actually a lengthy blank, about 133 centimetres (52⅜ inches) wide, where it is easy to see that the scroll has been reused and previous writing 'has been carefully erased and the papyrus buffed up again'.[50] As a result, the beginning of *The Teaching of Ptahhatp* obviously appears at the bottom of the fourth page, in a visual arrangement recognizably like the transition between chapters in a modern book (plate VI). *The Teaching of Ptahhatp* then continues until the end of the scroll—the fact that page nineteen is the actual end of *The Teaching* is clearly stated in red using a standard comment, 'so it ends, its start to its finish, as was found in writing'. The same comment signed by a scribe named Ameny'aa appears at the end of the only known copy of *The Story of the Shipwrecked Sailor*, which also came to light in the nineteenth century somewhere at Luxor.[51] An attractive observation is that the handwriting of the scribe of P.Prisse is very like that of Ameny'aa;[52] in other words, that he might have copied both *Shipwrecked Sailor* and P.Prisse before they were stored together in or near Dra' Abu al-Naga.

Papyrus London 1

A second copy of *The Teaching of Ptahhatp* from the late Middle Kingdom appears on the recto of the scroll known today as Papyrus London 1 (P.London 1).[53] The British Museum purchased this scroll in 1868 from Rollin & Feuardent—London-based dealers in 'coins, medals, gems, antiquities and numismatic books'—so nothing is known about where and how it was discovered, and it is in 'un état de mutilation déplorable', as Jéquier noted more than a century ago (plate II).[54] Apart from a few disconnected traces, the beginning is completely lost, presumably because the scroll had been rolled up in the usual manner with the initial pages on the outside, so the surviving text begins at what is already the very end of page five of *The Teaching* in P.Prisse. The hieratic hand is as clear and elegant as that of P.Prisse but the scribe has not used red ink anywhere other than the standard final comment identifying the book as a copy.

Interestingly, although the pages of P.London 1 are the same height as those of P.Prisse, *The Teaching* has been copied in the supposedly archaic style, using columns of writing. The Old Kingdom was the last time columns were ordinarily used in cursive documents, which may suggest that P.London 1 is 'the certainly oldest copy' of *The Teaching*.[55] In truth, this is far from certain: it may just as easily suggest that it is an exact facsimile of a much older scroll, now lost, or simply that it is intended to appear archaic. More to the point, we noted that P.Prisse, though written in lines, might well have been copied by the scribe Ameny'aa, who did copy *The Story of the Shipwrecked Sailor* using a combination of columns and lines. Indeed, switching between lines and columns might have been a characteristic practice in copying literature at this early time[56] — in truth we have too few examples to draw firm conclusions. As a final note, a group of otherwise unrelated administrative documents and accounts has been copied on the verso of P.London 1 — how long afterwards? — using horizontal lines in the ordinary 'contemporary' fashion.

Carnarvon Tablet 1

About 1500 BC, perhaps a century or two after P.Prisse and P.London 1 were written out, a scribe at the beginning of the Eighteenth Dynasty copied the beginning of *The Teaching of Ptahhatp* on one side of a plastered writing board known today as Carnarvon Tablet 1. This was found by Howard Carter (later to discover Tutankhamun's tomb) in 1908 among loose debris from a tomb at Deyr al-Bahari, and is now stored in Cairo.[57] At 25 centimetres (9⅞ inches) the board is much taller than the earlier papyrus copies but only 51 centimetres (20 inches) wide, so its seven-and-a-bit elegantly spaced lines, written in a single column using

The Prologue from *The Teaching of Ptahhatp* on Carnarvon Tablet 1,
possibly copied as writing practice. The grid sketched beneath it
is a game board with no obvious connection to the text.

a very rounded hand, only give the text as far as the middle of page two
in P.Prisse.[58] On the other side of the writing board, the same scribe
has copied out part of a monumental inscription that stood in the main
temple of the god Amun-Ra at Karnak in Thebes and had been composed
for Kamose, the last king of the Seventeenth Dynasty.

Papyrus London 2

From later in the Eighteenth Dynasty we have Papyrus London 2
(P.London 2),[59] which has been in the British Museum since 1899 but
was initially purchased by Chauncey Murch, an American Presbyterian
missionary based in Luxor from 1883 until his death in 1907.[60] P.London 2
has six complete pages plus the broken remnants of three more (bits
of which later turned up in Sir Alan Gardiner's private collection) and
seems to have originated in an ancient collection of 'several magnificent
literary books',[61] the rest of which were purchased in Luxor and are now

in the Pushkin Museum, Moscow. Sadly, once again nothing is known about this fine collection—where it came from or the circumstances of its discovery. However, befitting its distinguished character, P.London 2 is about 30 centimetres (12 inches) high because the New Kingdom scribe used a whole new scroll rather than half of one, presumably intending to create a 'magnificent' copy using a strong, clear hand—for whatever putative reason we may suggest. The scroll begins with a blank sheet, indicating that its beginning is intact (plate VII); then five complete pages of sixteen or seventeen lines each give *The Teaching of Ptahhatp* from the beginning to what is the top of page eight in P.Prisse, though with some teachings presented in a different order; and finally three more threadbare, very fragmentary pages get us as far as the middle of page fifteen of P.Prisse. This copy uses rubrics much more frequently than P.Prisse, as well as frequent red points above the lines, perhaps made by a reader rather than the copyist in order to bookmark or learn key sections of information.[62]

Papyrus Turin CGT 54014

Finally, moving forward a century or more to the Twentieth Dynasty, in the twelfth century BC, the beginning of *The Teaching of Ptahhatp* also appears on the recto of a scroll now in the Museo Egizio, Turin.[63] Just two fragments from what would seem to be the first written page are all that is known to survive, though these are sufficient to indicate that the scroll had the standard height of P.Prisse and the page accordingly has thirteen lines, written in a very clear hieratic hand.[64] Like P.London 2 it has rubrics and red points, presumably for the same reasons, though the surviving text is too brief to be certain about anything. This most recent copy is presumed to have come from the New Kingdom village at Deyr al-Medinah on the West Bank of Thebes (see page 34), though even this much is not certainly known; however, three contemporary ostraca quoting very brief extracts from the beginning of *The Teaching* certainly did come from there.[65]

*

The very first lines are all that survive of *The Teaching of Ptahhatp* on Papyrus Turin CGT 54014 (the verso is blank). About 15 cm (6 in.) high. Twentieth Dynasty. Probably Deyr al-Medinah.

Having considered all the manuscripts, we can note that P.Prisse does contain the only complete text of *The Teaching of Ptahhatp* (in sixteen pages) but that P.London 2 is complete from the beginning to what is the top of page eight of P.Prisse; by which point P.London 1 has entered the conversation because it includes the rest, from page six of P.Prisse to the end. So, as it transpires, we have multiple copies of the complete text of *The Teaching of Ptahhatp*, and there are significant differences between the manuscripts—not only specific words but even the order of the individual teachings. They are sufficiently different from one another to indicate that alternative text traditions are at play, so there is no reason to presume that any of the copies need be considered the original or best version. In other words, we use P.Prisse as the standard in modern times because it is complete in itself, a convenience caused by the vagaries of preservation. That said, there is a much more important observation to make: the texts of P.London 1, P.London 2 and Carnarvon Tablet 1 are strikingly similar to P.Prisse—sufficiently so to confirm that *The Teaching of Ptahhatp* is an authentic book, not simply the traditional, wistful attribution of any collection of wise sayings to the name Ptahhatp.

Even older books?

On the other hand, if *The Teaching of Ptahhatp* is a book, it is a book that has come down to us from the late Middle Kingdom—not from the reign of King Izezi in the Fifth Dynasty, almost a millennium earlier. In other words, is it really the 'oldest book', even from Egypt? We may readily assume that there must have been many lost literary 'classics' from ancient Egypt even older than P.Prisse—but the facts do not necessarily support this assumption. For example, if we were to consider possible authors in terms of the men mentioned in our eulogy of writers (see page 30), then Khety, Ptahemdhuty and Khakheperrasonb all lived after Ptahhatp, while Neferty we shall discuss below in a moment (see page 59); Kairsu is otherwise unknown and, though Imhotep is presumably the iconic vizier of King Netjerkhet Djoser of the Third Dynasty, not a trace of either man's writing has survived unless (unbeknown to us) Imhotep or

Kairsu is the unnamed author of *The Teaching of Kagemni*, which happens to be set during the Third Dynasty (see page 131); nowadays Hordedef tends to be identified (though on no secure basis) as a son of the Fourth Dynasty king Khufu (see page 136). Consequently, both *The Teaching of Kagemni* and *The Teaching of Hordedef* could be older compositions than Ptahhatp's—and what remains of them has also been translated in Chapter 3—but *Kagemni* is only known from P.Prisse in any event, while no more than the beginning of *Hordedef* has survived, and that in extracts written centuries after P.Prisse.

Speaking more broadly, we do have monumental inscriptions from temples taking us back to the beginning of Egyptian history, very roughly about 3000 BC, and we have royal funerary texts that are equally as ancient. The scribe Ahmose, who wrote the Rhind Mathematical Papyrus in the sixteenth century BC, noted that he was copying an older book written during the reign of Amenemhat III in the nineteenth century BC; and, as we noted above, the mathematics it exemplifies may well date back many centuries earlier. Another enormously important book in the Museo Egizio contains a detailed list of every king of Egypt down to the time it was written (during the reign of Ramesses II in the thirteenth century BC) and beginning, as the ancients understood matters, at the very birth of the world.[66] Again, it is easy to suppose that the scribe of this king-list relied on older books that by chance have not survived; although he might well have used other kinds of sources, such as the Palermo Stone mentioned in Chapter 2. We even have, still in our possession, personal letters written to the living and even to the dead during the Sixth Dynasty, almost forty-five centuries ago, including an angry letter from the army commander Meryranakht also discussed in Chapter 2. Nonetheless, we must be careful not to make too many assumptions about the ancient world: there is a species of cultural appropriation that fills in the considerable gaps in our knowledge by assuming that every culture must be essentially like our own at the end of the day. This may well seem charitable and inclusive, but are we not just planting our own flag in foreign soil? For example, the presumption that there is bound to have been a pervasive culture of books in any literate

Part of an allegorical tale about Snofru, King Khufu's father, and a magician
named Djadjamankh, from the first modern publication of Papyrus Westcar.
33.5 cm (1 ft 1¼ in.) high. Late Middle Kingdom.

society is not so clear-cut as we may assume today, in an age when the ubiquitous novel (or its television adaptation) seems to be the very life-blood of culture, high-brow and low-brow alike—especially bearing in mind that the majority of everything that has ever been written down has been written down in our lifetimes. As it happens, despite the fact that the Egyptians of all people evidently had the wherewithal to write books much earlier, there is not a scrap of literature that we can insist is older than *The Teaching of Ptahhatp*—and this may not be by chance.

The first group of ancient Egyptian literary books discovered in modern times, perhaps a decade before Prisse d'Avennes made his own momentous purchase, consisted of five scrolls obtained at Luxor in uncertain circumstances by Dimitrios Papandriopoulos (1798–1854)—a Greek-born Egyptian merchant and public servant, who styled himself Giovanni d'Athanasi. His 'very magnificent and extraordinary collection of Egyptian antiquities'[67] was sold over the course of an entire week in 1837 by Sotheby's Auctioneers in London, as a result of which four of the books made their way to the former Königliche Museen in Berlin.[68] The fifth book had been sold at auction two years previously and was subsequently bought by the British Museum from the Bishop of Lichfield in 1840. Like P.Prisse, these five books may be dated to the late Middle Kingdom, in the eighteenth or seventeenth century BC, and, indeed, it is far from improbable that P.Prisse is somehow linked to this collection.

A book that turned up on its own, and turned out to be the only extant copy of a tale about King Khufu and his sons (plate XVIII), was acquired in even more obscure circumstances in the late 1830s by the brilliant Prussian scholar Karl Richard Lepsius (1810–1884).[69] He donated the book to the Königliche Museen but today it is usually referred to as Papyrus Westcar after an even earlier owner, at least so the story goes —Henry Westcar, an Englishman who had travelled through Egypt as early as 1823–24. On the basis of its handwriting style, Papyrus Westcar is conventionally dated to the sixteenth century BC.[70]

Presumably the Rhind Mathematical Papyrus (see page 27) was part of another collection—in this instance a collection of more obviously technical books, including the celebrated Edwin Smith Medical Papyrus (now in New York[71]) and Ebers Medical Papyrus (now in Leipzig[72]), which were originally purchased on the West Bank at Luxor in 1862, reputedly having been found together in a tomb there.[73] These books are also dated to the sixteenth century BC.

In 1860 a pair of scrolls containing palace records and accounts, now in Cairo,[74] was collected by the Cairo-based archaeologist Auguste Mariette (1821–1881) from a tomb at Draʿ Abu al-Naga,[75] where they had been placed in a box alongside grave goods made for a royal scribe named Neferhotep. These books can be dated to the late eighteenth or seventeenth century BC.[76]

Finally, in 1896 the British archaeologist James Quibell (1867–1935) uncovered the single largest collection of books with literature from a very early date—a box containing perhaps two dozen scrolls in a late Middle Kingdom tomb on the West Bank of Thebes, lost beneath the granaries of a much later mortuary temple built for King Ramesses II (see page 34).[77] The box was evidently part of the burial, with an image of the funerary god Anubis sketched on the lid; and the books include literature, comparative word-lists, instructions for medical procedures and religious rituals, along with administrative documents, accounts and official letters, some of which have been copied incidentally 'on the back' (the versos).[78] The owner of this tomb has been fancifully characterized as a magician, though a more meaningful description is that he might have been a lector priest or an embalmer/undertaker.

Apart from these collections it is remarkable how little else by way of early books has survived, so even this brief summary is sufficient to demonstrate that the first appearance of literature in books is a *very specific* archaeological phenomenon in Egypt.[79] Consequently, there seems little doubt that P.Prisse was filched for sale from a Theban tomb, and that its survival is symptomatic of the patchy but not-at-all random pattern of preservation of early books. Not one book survives that was written down earlier than P.Prisse; and every book of this early date that we have today, a few fragments notwithstanding, came to light during the nineteenth century AD, having been collected in uncertain circumstances or discovered in tombs on the West Bank at Luxor. In fact, the total number of more-or-less intact literary texts written in the books that survive from this initial phase of production during the late Middle Kingdom is five, or maybe six if we include Papyrus Westcar.[80] The number we have in multiple copies is just three—two stories (*The Tale of the Eloquent Peasant*, *The Tale of Sinuhe*) and *The Teaching of Ptahhatp*. To these we can add the end of *The Teaching of Kagemni* in P.Prisse and bits of perhaps ten other texts in books, or fragments of books, found at Thebes or on a much smaller scale during excavations in contemporary cemeteries in Middle Egypt. Following this initial phase, we know of no other literature written before the New Kingdom—and even then only three significant collections of books have come down to us from some 500 years of the New Kingdom. To put this simply, the oldest two copies of *The Teaching of Ptahhatp* are demonstrably as old as the oldest books of literature to have survived.

Well, then, what about the possibility that *The Teaching of Ptahhatp* is actually no older than P.Prisse and P.London 1, its earliest manuscripts? In a sense, of course, this must be true—whatever we say about *The Teaching* prior to its first appearance in writing is more or less speculative. However, the full implication of this question is that: (a) there is no secure evidence that *The Teaching* existed at all before the earliest surviving copies, so (b) we should assume that the book did not exist before then. After all, pseudepigrapha—texts falsely attributed to an author taken from history—are an established phenomenon in ancient Egyptian literature. For example, take the story copied multiple times about a priest named Neferty, who makes a prophecy during the reign of King Snofru (in the Fourth Dynasty) about the accession of King Amenemhat I (in the Twelfth Dynasty)—but no modern commentator doubts that it was written after the fact of Amenemhat's accession.[81] In other words, the story's supposed antiquity is a plot device, and the date of its composition was much later than its setting—as late perhaps as the New Kingdom, when the earliest surviving copies were written down. The story also raises the possibility that the composer of our eulogy of ancient writers was fooled by the attribution because Neferty is one of the names he lauds alongside Ptahhatp. Of course, the composer might have had another text or another writer in mind; or the false attribution of a prophecy to Neferty might have come about precisely because he was already lauded for his wisdom. More to the point, Neferty's prophecy is presented within a narrative tale, whereas *The Teaching of Ptahhatp* is a fundamentally different kind of book—a series of statements ascribed to Ptahhatp, with a preface explaining how and why he spoke his Teaching before King Izezi.

In truth, the earliest manuscripts only give us a date when *The Teaching* already existed as a book—the dates of copies only tell us about the copies. To offer a comparison, much more recent books from history, including famous books by Aristotle, Julius Caesar and Marcus Aurelius, are barely known to us, if at all, in copies written before the second millennium AD, yet few scholars doubt their attribution to these otherwise well-known historical characters. By comparison, *The Teaching of Ptahhatp* is exceptionally well attested and, like these other men, Ptahhatp himself was once flesh and blood on this earth—not an evocative name on a page. Likewise, comparisons of the handwriting of manuscripts or the spellings of words may help us refine the dating of the copies—but not the date when the text was actually composed. This is another important point: for example, Miriam Lichtheim, a sympathetic interpreter of *The Teaching*, argued that 'the language of Kagemni and Ptahhotep is Middle Egyptian, the language of the Middle Kingdom'.[82] More recently, Stephen Quirke has highlighted the specific phrase 'staff of old age', used in the preface of *The Teaching*, which he sees as a Middle Kingdom turn of phrase, concluding:

> This term, the Middle Egyptian syntax and the late Middle Kingdom date of the two earliest surviving manuscript copies, point to a Twelfth Dynasty date of composition.[83]

As it happens, however, both these Egyptologists date the composition of *The Teaching* earlier than the oldest manuscripts—just not as early as the lifetime of Ptahhatp. The fact is that such arguments are circular insofar as we date changes in the language on the basis of the surviving documents—we do not have audio-recordings of how people actually spoke in the Old Kingdom. As a rule, monumental inscriptions from ancient Egypt tend to be more conservative in terms of the language they use than, for example, letters; yet there are monumental inscriptions from the Old Kingdom that are already written in Middle Egyptian, as Lichtheim for one concedes.[84] In fact, she actually attributes *The Teaching of Ptahhatp* to the Sixth Dynasty partly on this basis![85]

To pursue this point further, the language of the inscriptions in the tomb of Metjen from the early Fourth Dynasty, discussed in Chapter 2 —which are certainly among the very earliest monumental inscriptions in Egypt—can best be understood (in the opinion of the present author at least) as written in Middle Egyptian. If so, then the language of *The Teaching of Ptahhatp* is first attested before Ptahhatp lived in the Fifth Dynasty. Conversely, there are specific points of grammar in *The Teaching of Ptahhatp* that Egyptologists ordinarily ascribe only to the language of the Old Kingdom.[86] In other words, we cannot reasonably impose a hard-and-fast distinction between the language of *The Teaching* as we have it written down and the language we may suppose was spoken in the Egyptian palace community during the Fifth Dynasty. To be fair, it would hardly be contentious to suggest that *The Teaching* was possibly (probably?) composed in something of the formal, spoken language of the Old Kingdom palace, which in turn is reflected in the formal, literary language of the Middle Kingdom— and, to emphasize, there are no literary books older than P.Prisse to inform our thinking about this matter. As a simple matter of fact, written language in any literate culture tends to be more formal and normative than speech, which is why today when writing certain types of documents we use specific phrases we would probably not use freely in speaking, such as 'dear sir or madam' and 'yours faithfully'. To add a flippant example, I have seen the word 'scion' used frequently in academic writing but never yet met anyone who is confident about how to pronounce it—apparently never having heard the word spoken out loud.

More to the point, as Quirke has helpfully summarized, 'the copyists lead us into a world beyond the genesis of a composition, the world

The Fifth Dynasty was a watershed for the diffusion of writing throughout Egypt. Most dramatically, wall-to-wall monumental religious inscriptions appear in the tombs of kings for the first time, as the so-called 'Pyramid Texts' (see pages 94–95). Fifth Dynasty, tomb of King Wenis. Saqqara.

of its reception and dissemination in a society.'[87] As we now know, in the case of the earliest literary books this is not a wide dissemination; in fact, beyond being deposited in the tombs of a very small number of men, where and how these books were actually known and used is a matter for speculation. The unrelated administrative texts on the verso of P.London 1, or the copy of a royal inscription on the other side of Carnarvon Tablet 1, do allow the possibility that copies of *The Teaching* might have been employed for some indeterminate purpose in a scribe's office before they were finally interred in someone's tomb— though whether anything written on them was ever intended simply for the enjoyment of reading is a different issue. We must also be mindful of the depth of time in which the different text traditions of the earliest copies of *The Teaching* came about, even if we cannot be sure how deep this may be. Jéquier, for one, believed that the differences betray a tradition of oral transmission 'without attaching undue importance to copying the exact wording of the text'.[88] More recently the Egyptologist Alessandro Roccati has made the same point.[89] Whether or not there is a tradition of exact copying, in writing or in speaking, copyists do make alterations, intentionally or by mistake, and they can certainly update or 'editorialize' texts. So, once again, the language of copies only tells us about the dates of the copies.

Where does all this leave us, then? We can with justification assert that *The Teaching of Ptahhatp* is an authentic book, surviving in multiple copies, including two copies that are undoubtedly as old as the oldest books to have come down to us. Indeed, *The Teaching of Ptahhatp* is exceptionally well attested among the oldest surviving books. Along with this, we can note the ancient, native tradition that ascribes certain books to lauded authors whose personal reputations are integral to the authority of the book. One of these authors is Ptahhatp and there is not a single surviving book ascribed to a writer who might have lived before him, apart from the *The Teaching of Kagemni* also on P.Prisse and (possibly) the fragments of *The Teaching of Hordedef*. This tradition, of course, also serves to remind us that Ptahhatp was indeed a living, breathing human being who once walked this earth—so who was Ptahhatp?

2

THE OVERSEER OF THE CITY AND VIZIER, PTAHHATP

As everyone naturally desires to know, then they
desire most of all the best knowledge. ... That said,
there are two ways things can be said to be most knowable:
either they are the principles without which nothing
else can be known; or they are the facts that can be
learned with most certainty.[1]

JOHN DUNS SCOTUS (*c.* 1265–1308),
Direct Enquiries into Aristotle's Metaphysics, Prologue

ACCORDING TO *The Teaching*, Ptahhatp lived during the Old Kingdom. We would do well not to underestimate the hubris of the Old Kingdom, which was an exercise in transforming the human community on a scale never previously imagined. No doubt, as the Egyptologist Ludwig Morenz has summarized, 'the process of state formation in Egypt was ... very complex indeed, presumably involving factors such as trade, technologies, ideology, political ambition, media of communication, stratification of society'.[2] Quite so, but by the time of Ptahhatp in the mid-third millennium BC such matters were already treated by the people of Egypt as matters confined to the beginning of history, countless centuries earlier, when the nation's throne had first become the measure of good conduct as explained in Ptahhatp's Thirteenth Teaching. In every generation since, the pharaoh's authority over hearts and minds had extended into new areas. From the handful of tangible archaeological remains we may take the impression that the emphasis during Izezi's reign fell on building and redeveloping temples away from the nation's main population centre at Memphis, while at the same time inculcating the pharaonic cult of food-offerings for the dead in every regional cemetery. In truth, this impression, taken directly from the stone monuments, merely skates the surface of Egypt's earliest history: projects in our present generation creating cities out of forested mountains in China or the deserts and seas of Arabia seem derivative and insubstantial by comparison to the world's first great state-project, which resulted in more than eight centuries of political stability, economic prosperity and unprecedented cultural self-belief; but conversely had a devastating and so far irreversible impact on the fauna and flora of the River Nile, leading to the local extinction of many indigenous species.[3] These were not tentative, unthinking evolutionary steps by our simple-minded forebears but the mark of a self-assured, self-governed, imaginative nation making a conscious decision to transform the world around quite literally.[4]

For a single example let us also go back to the beginning of history. As Egyptologists or lovers of ancient Egypt we can get so accustomed to the countless tomb inscriptions of pharaonic officials across thousands of years that we forget there must have been a first one—and, arguably,

Giza and its pyramids during the Nile inundation.
At the time of this photograph, modern barrages were already managing
the river flow but the inundation was still overwhelming.

this is the decorated tomb-chapel of Metjen (plate III). This was stripped
out of its mastaba at Saqqara and removed to the Königliche Museen in
Berlin in 1843 as part of an expedition directed by the Prussian philologist
Karl Richard Lepsius.⁵ Its mastaba—by which we mean a tumulus built
of solid stone, mostly undecorated—stood about a quarter of a mile
(400 metres) north of the Step Pyramid enclosure, where it had become
buried in sand and consequently has been relatively well preserved (see
page 79). Concerning the chapel, Lepsius commented on the high quality
of the limestone and the detail in the hieroglyphs, which are mostly
'sharp, good and highly polished', whereas the relief work is 'cumbersome
and a bit lacking in style'.⁶ In truth, his judgment seems harsh and we

may presume that the tomb was decorated by the same small pool of master craftsmen responsible for the distinguished decorative work in the contemporary pyramid enclosures of Netjerkhet Djoser and Snofru, or the famous wooden panels from the mastaba tomb of the chief physician Hezyra.

An inscription at the entrance to Metjen's tomb-chapel, on the east side of the mastaba, announced a very narrow (0.67 metres or 2 feet) and high (2.52 metres or 8¼ feet) passageway, decorated with his biography written in columns of raised relief on both sides. For the roof, limestone blocks shaped as cedar logs ran lengthways along this passage, which opens into a transverse offering chamber. Here a window on the north side looks into a serdab, which is simply a stone box for Metjen's granite statue, about a quarter life-size (plate v);[7] by this time statues showing the deceased dressed in fine linen and carrying symbols of authority were already typical in the tombs of high officials. In the far west wall of this chamber—in effect, at the junction of the T-shaped chapel—is a deeply niched wall or 'false door' intended as the focus for offerings, and decorated with a prodigious statement of Metjen's achievements and extensive endowments of land, whereas the biography on the walls of the entrance passageway explains his success. This west wall also happens to mention his commitment to the funerary cult of Nyma'athep, great wife of Khasekhemwy, last king of the Second Dynasty—and presumably, therefore, the mother of Netjerkhet Djoser, whose pyramid Metjen was buried beside. On the other hand, the name of Snofru, first king of the Fourth Dynasty, appears above the window into Metjen's serdab, so Metjen presumably lived most of his life during the Third Dynasty and died while Snofru's multifarious collection of pyramids was under construction during the twenty-sixth century BC.

Here's the point. We may love watching television programmes about the relationship between these early people and the vast construction projects of the pyramids and sun-temples associated with them. We may even succumb to the extraordinary racism involved in ascribing preternatural knowledge to them—such as may be found in the 'Grand Copht' tradition of Freemasonry—or speculating whether ancient Africans required extra-terrestrial intervention to achieve as much as they did. However, in doing so we are still hugely underestimating the total scale of the urban industrial project the Egyptians were engaged in during the Old Kingdom.[8] Metjen's career, for instance, illustrates a more massive and enduring aspect of the project, and the aspect by which 'the floodplain-based fauna as well as the desert fauna and flora were substantially decimated':[9] while some of his fellows were indeed piling up stone for pyramids, and others were developing the urban sprawl of Memphis, Metjen became the go-to man of his age for hydraulic engineering, especially adept at managing the marshes and lands along the fringes of the Nile Delta to 'open it up' for agriculture and safe settlement. Safe, despite the formidable annual inundation of the Nile, when heavy rains across the East African highlands caused the river to rise every year from late June until it reached a peak in August, usually at least 1.5 metres (5 feet) higher at the entrance to the Delta than it began but frequently higher still. Because of this overwhelming volume, the inundation swept floodwater full of organic debris right through the valley to the edge of the desert cliffs, until the full load had to be discharged via the Nile Delta into the Mediterranean Sea. Consequently, at the beginning of the agricultural year the whole of Egypt was essentially a single body of water, cleansing the land and bringing soil wherever it reached, while anywhere beyond remained the barren Sahara Desert (see page 67). Dotted about in the floodwater were people's homes, workshops and farm buildings on patches of high ground called 'baskets' in ancient texts, as though they were bobbing about until the water retreated in October. According to the Palermo Stone, a fragmentary basalt stela that once summarized events in each year of the earliest kings, an especially high inundation during the First Dynasty reign of King Den—a rise of 'eight cubits and three fingers' (4.25 metres or 14 feet)—was disastrous and the following year's record simply reads 'across the west and east flooding (i.e. bursting) the watersheds of all the people'.[10] This was the Egypt where Metjen grew up—a vast, rich, fertile agricultural land perched every year on the brink of disaster.

In contemporary inscriptions (and in *The Teaching of Ptahhatp*), the Old Kingdom regime is presented as a meritocracy at least among the community that could hope to be known to the king—not, perhaps, among the majority population of farmers—and Metjen's biography is in accord. Early in his career he worked at 'Sinai Lake' and 'Southern Lake', possibly some of the natural lakes along the route of what is now the Suez Canal, and eventually was given responsibility for the communities at Dep, Buto, Xois, Sais, Mendes, Letopolis and elsewhere in the Nile Delta. He had a spell developing land at the western edge of the Delta along the 'Great Respect' canal, further spells reclaiming desert for settlement ('fields, watersheds, people and everything') and a spell managing the shifting sandbanks in the Nile itself. At one point he was assigned further south to Crocodilopolis, the largest settlement in the huge Faiyum oasis, developing wetlands on the lake side of that community. All of this, however, despite an unpromising coming-of-age, presumably in Xois, where his father left him 'neither wheat nor barley nor anything tangible for an estate but there were people and animals'. In modern terms, his father left him essentially only debts and responsibilities. Still, his father had been a 'superintendent of writing', so Metjen had one gift—he was steeped in this extraordinary new technology; so it was 'that he would be put in charge of writing in the provisions office as keeper of the business of the provisions office'. This would be his entry into public life but, as it happened, his chance to get noticed came during the boat festivals that were at the heart of these early Egyptian communities, when 'he would be put as a strong-oarsman and physician/coach for the stroke-rowers' . Metjen's prowess was such that even the local governor had to follow his lead. Afterwards 'he would be put as keeper of all the king's flax' and designated as 'staff-bearer'—a title which in turn becomes the iconic image of an Old Kingdom royal official. From this moment, an exceptional career was up and running. As the first part of his biography on the north side of the entrance passageway ends, a community named Sheret-Metjen 'was founded in front of what his father Anpumankh gave him', and Metjen is seen to have turned the pittance he inherited into an abundance. In a sense, he has become a symbol of the Old Kingdom Delta itself.

On the facing wall, Metjen is already a success and notes that 'stroke-rowers were assigned to him during his processions in western Sais as keeper of development'—once he had been a rower, now he was rowed. We learn that a dozen more communities were founded in his name near Sais, Xois and Letopolis; that he was awarded the serdab for his tomb; that 'two hundred arouras [*c.* 4.8 hectares] of fields were brought to him as a reward from various kings' and 'fifty arouras [*c.* 1.2 hectares] of fields were given to him for (his) mother, Netnebes'. Metjen acknowledged such beneficence in kind, and a hundred loaves went out every day from his mortuary foundation for the funerary offerings of the king's mother, Nyma'athep. The foundation itself is a little garden of paradise 'two hundred cubits long and two hundred cubits wide [*c.* 11,000 m² or 2¾ acres], stone-built and properly equipped, with perfect trees planted where there is a very large lake, and figs and grapes also planted'. Other, larger endowments are recorded and the inscriptions take pains on three occasions to confirm that the relevant land documents exist (among his family but also, of course, among his literate peers) to give detailed breakdowns of his endowments.

Interestingly, land documents of this kind have been copied onto the walls of other early tombs, confirming the reality of this sophisticated legal activity. For example, a wall in the tomb of Nykawira at Giza[11] has been inscribed with a copy of his testament confirming donations of land—mostly in a city built as part of the development of the pyramid enclosure of his father, King Khafra—as funerary endowments for other people, just like those his royal forefathers granted to Metjen. A contemporary stela, whose owner's name is lost,[12] specifically states that no one is legally allowed to transfer such funerary endowments to anyone else:

> I do not authorize any mortuary priest at any time to give away the land, people or anything else that I have made as a funerary offering from me to them by transaction with any person, whether through giving or through a will for anyone other than their children, etc.

Actual scrolls detailing similar legal endowments along with copies of royal commands 'signed before the king himself' have even been found

Metjen's final trip into the western desert. Scene covering three walls of his
tomb-chapel, with offerings to his serdab statue represented at top (see plate v).
Fourth Dynasty. Saqqara.

among assorted duty rosters, inventories of equipment and records of deliveries of goods in the mortuary temples of two kings and a queen of the Fifth Dynasty.[13]

What is most striking amid such detail is how closely Metjen's tomb-chapel conforms to later tombs from pharaonic Egypt, as though the unwavering template for success has already been set out at this early date: such hubris, as we noted above! His earthly paradise with a garden lake is effectively reproduced in tomb paintings for the next 2,000 years, the overall scheme of decoration is wholly accomplished in conception and execution, and the texts are extensive and elegantly composed. That said, Metjen's story may be summarized in a single scene from the offering chapel: we see him leading an expedition into the desert, complete with hunting dogs, a tent and a cooking pot. He also brings with him the defining mark of civilization — portable toilet facilities because, of course, humans are least like animals when engaged with our biological functions. In life, Metjen knew well this treacherous journey into a seemingly lifeless desert; and here, in the tomb, he is asked to make one final trek to the west. As a man who had made marshes and deserts bloom for kings and their subjects — a man who had turned an empty inheritance into a dozen new communities bearing his own name — this last expedition is surely bound to succeed. Above this scene, his serdab statue is shown receiving the offerings that on the opposite walls are brought to him from the very communities that carry his name. As a man who served, with exceptional effectiveness, the king laid to rest in the Step Pyramid next door, Metjen surely expected to be wanted in the kingdom that is the next life but, equally, to be remembered in the nation he had literally helped to form. Today, however, as a man who turned the gift of literacy into an exemplary career, his tomb-chapel stands as a first, glorious celebration of this new, transformative technology — transformative in terms of its impact on one man's life but, more fundamentally, in terms of drawing back the curtain across history for the first time, to illuminate the sense of ourselves as named individuals within communities over time on this earth.

Ptahhatp and Izezi

Ptahhatp is presented to us in *The Teaching* as a historical character—the senior figure at the court of Izezi (r. *c.* 2410–2375 BC), a Fifth Dynasty king who, according to later records, reigned somewhere between twenty-eight and forty-four years. However far distant these people may seem in the past, the tombs of both the king and his most trusted official may still be visited in the great royal cemetery at Saqqara, near modern Cairo. The ruinous pyramid enclosure of Izezi himself sits at the far south of Saqqara, on high ground after which locals have named it

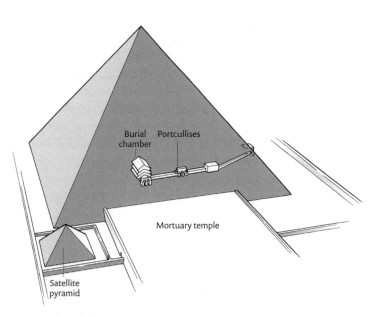

King Izezi's pyramid (ABOVE), with a burial chamber cut into the desert floor, has a standard layout but many innovative features. For the first time, the king's principal wife has a duplicate pyramid complex (OPPOSITE).

al-Shawaf, 'the Look-out' (see page 79). The site has been systematically surveyed only during the last decade but originally the pyramid stood more than 50 metres (170 feet) high, bore the name 'Izezi is perfected' (see page 192) and incorporated innovative architecture that would remain standard in royal pyramids for the remainder of the Old Kingdom.[14] Today, nothing beside remains, at least not above the level of the limestone pavements in its once beautiful temples, apart from the smaller, equally ruinous pyramid built for his Great Wife, Herusetibi—the first queen of this era to be accorded her own pyramid complex instead of a subsidiary burial within her king's enclosure.[15]

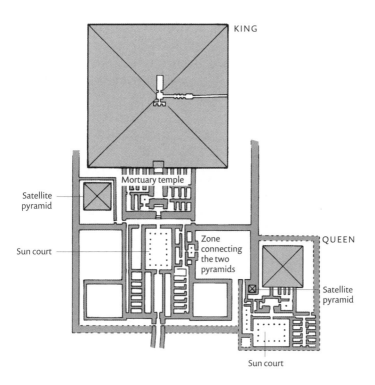

KING

Mortuary temple

Satellite pyramid

Sun court

Zone connecting the two pyramids

QUEEN

Satellite pyramid

Sun court

Part of a relief scene depicting Merertizezi, 'the king's daughter of his body'
(see page 81) and a member of his entourage. Limestone.
53 cm (1 ft 8¾ in.) high. Fifth Dynasty. Abusir.

Likewise, on the basis of the scant remains of contemporary monu-ments we can say little more about Izezi's family.[16] Even his relationship to his predecessors as king, Nyuserra and Menkauhoru, is unknown. Three sons of a king buried beside one another in tombs along the north wall of the Step Pyramid may be his sons insofar as one is named Izeziankhu, which means 'Izezi is alive'.[17] He rose to be Overseer of All the King's Building,[18] and his brothers were Ramkai[19] and Kaimtjenenet.[20] Accordingly, the king's wife Meresankh, whose tomb is also here,[21] may be their mother and another wife of Izezi. While we cannot be certain that these people are Izezi's family, by chance his daughter Merertizezi (whose name means 'she whom Izezi loves') may be seen today in the Brooklyn Museum on a fragment of decorated limestone from a lost tomb or temple.[22]

Ptahhatp's tomb is at Saqqara too,[23] beside the northwest corner of the Step Pyramid enclosure, prominent among a complex of mastabas dating from the reign of Izezi[24] and in sight of the tombs of Izeziankhu and his brothers (plate x). More precisely, this is the mastaba tomb of Ptahhatp, the first vizier or prime minister of King Izezi. In truth, there are tombs at Saqqara for five different viziers named Ptahhatp[25] — but only one fits the bill. Another Ptahhatp, for example, was also vizier for Izezi but easily outlived him, so he can hardly be the venerable old man of *The Teaching* (plate xi).[26] In fact, he was the grandson of the first Ptahhatp, so let us call these men Ptahhatp (I) and Ptahhatp (II). The other three viziers named Ptahhatp held office during the Fifth Dynasty or Sixth Dynasty but we do not know which kings they served. This may seem an unlikely coincidence until we appreciate a couple of facts: that high offices were often inherited, so all five Ptahhatps could well be members of the same family; and that the practice of retaining a name within a family was common enough at this time.

To take this conundrum step by step, we may begin by numbering our viziers from Ptahhatp (I) to Ptahhatp (V) — purely for the sake of clarity, because we cannot be sure of the exact order in which they lived and served.[27] We know that Ptahhatp (I) is the first vizier of Izezi and that Ptahhatp (II) is his grandson, who outlived Izezi. We do not know of any relationship between these men and Ptahhatp (III) and Ptahhatp (IV), but the tombs of the last two stand next to one another much further north than the Step Pyramid—in a cemetery near the pyramids of kings earlier in the Fifth Dynasty.[28] Ptahhatp (V) was buried in an impressive tomb to the south of the pyramid of King Wenis, which in turn is on the far side of the Step Pyramid from any of the tombs noted above.[29] We do not know this man's relationship to the other four Ptahhatps.

We do not know which kings Ptahhatp (III), Ptahhatp (IV) and Ptahhatp (V) served, so could one of them be our man instead? Yes, of course, but we also know that Izezi had five other viziers between Ptahhatp (I) and Ptahhatp (II), none of whom was named Ptahhatp.[30] One of Izezi's other viziers was Akhethatp, the son of Ptahhatp (I) and father of Ptahhatp (II). Another vizier, Seshemnefer, was one of Ptahhatp's mortuary priests and might have been a relative, while yet another, Snedjemib-Inti, might have been married into his family.[31] So, Izezi's known viziers include three generations of one family during a reign of forty-four years or less, and there are at least four other viziers to weave into this succession.[32] In other words, after Ptahhatp (I) there seems no room to introduce another aged vizier named Ptahhatp. We can much more straightforwardly presume that Ptahhatp (III), Ptahhatp (IV) and Ptahhatp (V) served other kings in the Fifth or Sixth Dynasties than add them to the long list of Izezi's viziers[33]—especially if any of them belongs to yet another generation of the family of Ptahhatp (I), his son Akhethatp and his grandson Ptahhatp (II). For instance, the location of the cemetery in which Ptahhatp (III) and Ptahhatp (IV) were buried may suggest a relationship with earlier kings (Mariette placed them in the Fourth Dynasty[34]), whereas Ptahhatp (I), Akhethatp and Ptahhatp (II) were buried in a cemetery certainly begun in the reign of Izezi and situated near that of Izezi's putative sons.[35]

OPPOSITE Sketch plan of the royal cemeteries at Saqqara showing the relative locations of various places mentioned in the text.

78

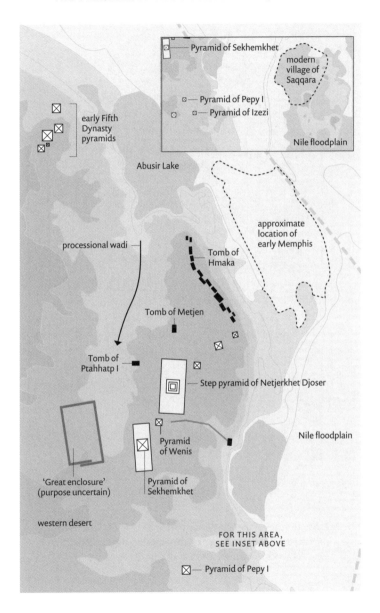

Pyramid of Sekhemkhet

modern village of Saqqara

Pyramid of Pepy I
Pyramid of Izezi

Nile floodplain

early Fifth Dynasty pyramids

Abusir Lake

approximate location of early Memphis

processional wadi

Tomb of Hmaka

Tomb of Metjen

Tomb of Ptahhatp I

Step pyramid of Netjerkhet Djoser

Nile floodplain

Pyramid of Wenis

'Great enclosure' (purpose uncertain)

Pyramid of Sekhemkhet

western desert

FOR THIS AREA, SEE INSET ABOVE

Pyramid of Pepy I

Mariette's copy of the false door in the tomb-chapel of Ptahhatp (I).
A 'false door' is actually a stone niche emulating the outside walls
of a palace or temple. Original 2.38 m (7 ft 9¾ in.) high.

At this point, some readers will insist, quite correctly, that we cannot prove Ptahhatp (I) is the aged vizier of *The Teaching*. To which charge one could only respond that, after 4,500 years, is it not truly remarkable to have a candidate from history so strong as Ptahhatp, the first vizier of Izezi? Of course, we could argue that *The Teaching* need not have been written by any actual vizier named Ptahhatp: it could well have been written by someone else altogether and credited to an invented vizier Ptahhatp, but which sceptical rabbit hole is that going to lead us down? Perhaps your own answer to the question 'is vizier Ptahhatp (I) the author of *The Teaching*?' ultimately depends on whether you are willing to believe that an ancient book is what it says it is when there is good evidence to support the claim, or whether your scepticism will only countenance what can be proved beyond any shadow of a doubt, even after the passage of four and a half millennia.

That said, there does seem to be one compelling objection to this identification: in *The Teaching* Ptahhatp is said to be 'king's eldest son of his body', which is the standard way of stating that he is the biological son of a king. Given Ptahhatp's old age and the principle of father–son succession, the king in question can hardly be Izezi himself, which may lead us to presume that he is from an earlier generation — Izezi's uncle or great uncle perhaps. On the other hand, a full statement of the titles of the vizier Ptahhatp (I) appears on a false door in his tomb-chapel and he is decidedly *not* a king's son. All this said, the inconsistency is more apparent than real — because the Ptahhatp of *The Teaching* was never a king's son either. First of all, there are several other instances — specifically during the Fifth Dynasty — of this title being held as an honour by viziers who were not the biological sons of any king. More to the point, P.Prisse, P.London 2 and Carnarvon Tablet 1 all begin with a list of Ptahhatp's titles, which is the same list in each case and does not identify him as a king's son. The same list is repeated later in the book — at the beginning of the actual teachings — at which point P.London 2 interpolates the title 'judge in the six great temples' whereas P.Prisse alone interpolates 'king's eldest son of his body'. In other words, the use of this phrase is the contribution of a copyist, editorializing his text through some creative interpretation of who Ptahhatp might have been —perhaps realizing that the title was typical for a vizier in the late Old Kingdom, or perhaps on the presumption that he ought to have been a king's son like, for instance, Hordedef. In any event, a single emendation among multiple copies is insufficient reason to prevent us identifying the vizier Ptahhatp (I) with *The Teaching of Ptahhatp*.

So, in *The Teaching* Ptahhatp is said to be Vizier, in effect the prime minister who runs the government while the king leads the nation in worship and the festivals of the gods; and a community-leader, in effect, the mayor or governor of one of Egypt's districts—a position that had recently been created by combining the office of controller of agricultural activity and leader of the main temple estate in most districts. He is also said to belong to the *pa'at*, the select group of advisers who surrounded the king, literally and practically. He is titled Overseer of the City, meaning that he was the project manager for the construction of the king's pyramid enclosure—the 'City' in question being both the building site and the infrastructure that supported it. Finally, he is the God's Father and the God's Beloved—titles that relate him personally to the divine king (the 'God'), not least because the title God's Father probably denotes a man involved in the education of the new king. Each of these titles or meaningful equivalents also appears in the vizier's tomb-chapel, along with many of the highest administrative titles of the period, including Overseer of All the King's Business, Keeper of Secrets for the King, Keeper of Secrets for Every Chamber of the King, Overseer of All the King's Building, Overseer of the Twin Treasuries and Overseer of the Twin Granaries ('twin' because royal estates were divided between providing for the palaces and feasting royal officials on the one hand and providing for the king's family, his pyramid enclosure and his religious endowments on the other[36]). In the area of literacy specifically, Ptahhatp in his tomb is titled Chief Lector Priest, God's Scribe and Overseer for Writing the King's Documents—in fact, in the very chapel with the false door he is also depicted supervising the writing of the king's documents.

Whereas we noted in the last chapter that *The Teaching of Ptahhatp* is authentically a book ascribed in ancient times to a historical author,

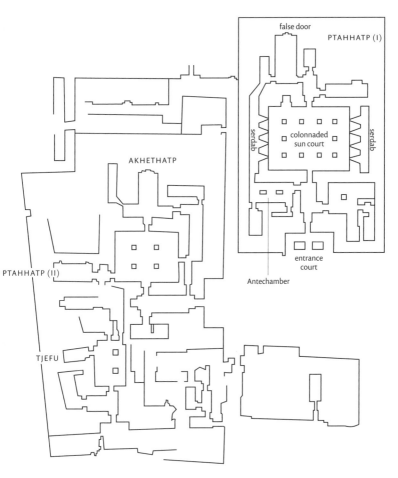

Plan of the complex of tomb-chapels for the family of Ptahhatp (I),
including his son Akhethatp and grandsons Ptahhatp (II) and Tjefu.
His own tomb is the largest and most elaborate. Fifth Dynasty. Saqqara.

there seems little reason to doubt which historical person the author is. Though Ptahhatp's mastaba tomb, almost 20 metres (64 feet) square and made of huge limestone blocks, was ruinous when discovered in the nineteenth century, Mariette could still praise it for its unusual arrangement of rooms and 'especially for the perfection of the reliefs which decorate the main room'.[37] It subsequently became the first tomb in a cemetery for at least three further generations of his relatives: Akhethatp's tomb is next door, now joined to that of Ptahhatp (II).[38] Such Old Kingdom tombs were not simply satellites round the kings' pyramids; each is a place of worship in its own right, overlooking the routes of religious festival processions. Accordingly, Ptahhatp's chapel is intended as a public area, not a burial place (the dark, undecorated burial chamber was cut into the desert beneath the tomb floor); first and foremost a chapel for visiting, remembering and offering to the deceased's immortal presence or 'spirit' (*ka*) — a word we will discuss further in Chapter 4. The inscriptions at the door are now broken but would have asked passers-by to stop and remember Ptahhatp after the fashion of the invitation above the entrance to the tomb-chapel of the palace's chief draughtsman and festival priest, Nedjemib:[39]

> Make me an offering from what you brought with you: I am one whom people have loved. I have never been punished in the presence of any official from the time I was born, and never taken the property of anyone as a robber. I am one who has done what everyone respects.[40]

The entrance leads you from an open court through a small, dark room to a sunlit colonnaded court. Along both the north and south walls of Ptahhatp's courtyard are four pairs of windows for viewing and censing statues of him in serdabs. Whereas the serdabs on the north were sealed, two wooden statues discovered in this area might have been part of a group from the southern serdabs,[41] which could be entered from an ante-chamber to dress the statues during the same ritual purification applied each day to the statues of every god in every temple in Egypt (plate XIII).

Beyond the colonnaded court on the far west of the tomb lies the suite of pitch-dark rooms where food-offerings were made by oil lamp for the spirit or presence of Ptahhatp during the religious festivals—presumably in front of one or more stone statues of the Vizier, long since lost but just like the seated statue of Metjen. The largest of these rooms (the very one praised by Mariette) has the decorated false door as the main focus for offerings. The walls of this space are also decorated with scenes of people bringing offerings to the tomb from thirty estates named for Ptahhatp as well as for various kings, and archaeological finds nearby such as a jar-stopper or clay seals may be the surviving traces of such offerings.[42] A list of the priests for his funerary cult takes up a whole wall and includes members of his family, and the later vizier Seshemnefer, who carries the family cognomen Tjefu. Here we also see Ptahhatp's sons, Ptahhatp and, of course, Akhethatp, who later served as the first overseer of the entire Nile Valley—which was one of Izezi's principal government reforms—and eventually succeeded his father as vizier. Both are shown as children but, sadly, only Akhethatp appears as an adult—he is the scribe registering the offerings brought to his father's tomb—so the other son might well have predeceased his father. Poignantly the introduction of *The Teaching* in P.London 2 (not the earlier copies) is addressed 'to little Ptahhatp'.

Wisdom and literacy

From the moment it was composed *The Teaching of Ptahhatp* was intended to embody the authority of age and pass on wisdom that has stood the test of time, whether we ascribe that authority to Ptahhatp himself or to a fictional setting in 'olden days'. According to the text, however, he is a man of 110 years old, an aspirational age in Egyptian funerary texts, after a lifetime of service to his kings. Through age and service, Ptahhatp has come to embody the knowledge and conduct that is consistent with truth, following the ancient belief that wisdom, because it is founded in spiritual growth, may reach its peak decades after the body's physical and mental faculties have begun their terminal decline. Rightly or wrongly, this is a very different conception than that of a culture today which reduces mental and spiritual capacity to a function of the brain

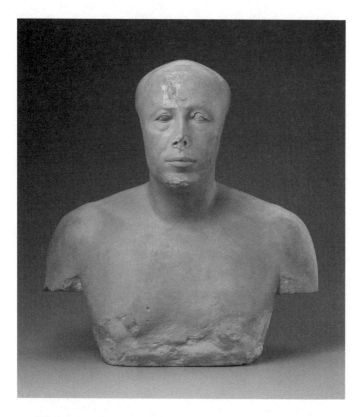

Ankhhaf, vizier and Overseer of All the King's Building, from his tomb-chapel.
The 'bust' might have been provided with outstretched arms to receive offerings.
Plastered limestone. 51 cm (1 ft 8 in.) high. Fourth Dynasty. Giza.

and measures maturity in reproductive terms. Indeed, Ptahhatp begins
his spoken testament by summarizing his own physical decline, lamenting that 'what old age does to people is wicked in every way', before the
younger king asks him to write down all that he has learned.

Accordingly, if we were to try to picture Ptahhatp in the round, we
may well recall the limestone statue of Ankhhaf in the Museum of Fine
Arts, Boston,[43] a slightly earlier vizier and the man responsible for

overseeing the projects to build the Great Pyramid of Khufu as well as the pyramid and Great Sphinx for King Khafra.[44] From his tomb at Giza,[45] the statue is a most accomplished and affecting illustration of aged flesh: the pronounced bone structure of his face contrasts with the flaccid skin round his eyes and cheeks and the lines round his nose and lips to create, like Ptahhatp, a harsh account of ageing. Likewise, the vizier Hemiunu, probably another project-manager for the Great Pyramid, was certainly a member of the royal family and one of the most dignified people of his day; but in his tomb statue, now in Hildesheim, we cannot ignore the pendulous breasts of a corpulent, older man nor the rolls of abdominal flab and the flaccid belly (plate XIV).[46] In other words, the leading officials of the Old Kingdom in the hands of the culture's most accomplished artists have statues that highlight the morbidity of flesh precisely because physical decay is an indicator of increasing knowledge and wisdom. Art in an Old Kingdom tomb-chapel illustrates the authority of the spirit—what the novelist John Steinbeck called the human 'creative instrument'. Hence their statues defy modern expectations of strength and physical perfection, which today may require cosmetic surgery, improbable claims to infallibility, and even the downright denial of mortality—but what do we know of the meaning of life, if our only purpose is to stay alive?

The Old Kingdom artists developed another image that also draws us towards Ptahhatp: the royal official as a writer, like the anonymous official in a celebrated statue discovered by Mariette at Saqqara.[47] The scribe sits with his knees extended to unroll the book in his left hand, the fingers of his right hand poised as though gripping a reed brush. We could just as easily visualize him—a career politician—with a laptop or tablet instead, which may create a more authentic sense of the statue's original impact. Writing kept an official close to the king even when separated in space just as, at Saqqara again, a royal companion named Djadjamankh describes himself on his false door as 'one who does everything commanded to him from the very moment of writing' and, therefore, 'one who is in the thoughts of his lord because very truly he fulfils the king's wishes with everything he wants'.[48] A magnificent

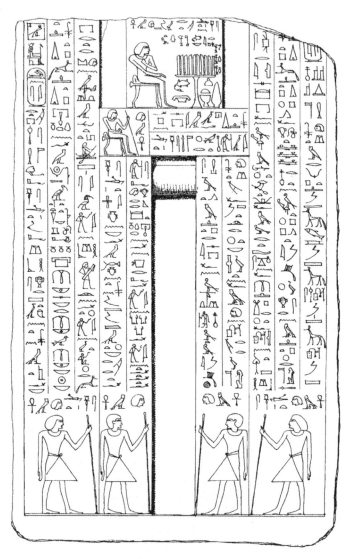

Mariette's copy of the false door in the tomb-chapel of Djadjamankh.
Original 3.3 m (10 ft 10 in.) high.

false door made for Nyankhsakhmet, an overseer of palace physicians, relates how the false door came to be made, including the fact that even the writing was King Sahura's gift to his official:

> So his person had a stone doorway brought to him from Turah-quarry and put for me in the very audience-room of the palace named 'Sahura appears in the great crown'. A chief mason and masons of the purification-room were set to it, and the work was done by them beside the king himself. The stone took shape each day and what they did was seen by the assembled court throughout the day. Then his person had inscriptions cut from it for me, and they were written in blue.[49]

Certain Egyptologists now question whether or not there is even a direct correspondence between the word we translate as 'scribe' (*zesha'*) and the concept of literacy as such, suggesting that the word may be more to do with 'penmanship' as a skill, denoting a copyist and little more.[50] Nevertheless, the careers and tombs of Metjen, Ptahhatp and their peers unequivocally demonstrate the inherent authority of those who could manipulate this technology during the Old Kingdom. Royal letters copied out as inscriptions round the entrance to the tomb of the vizier Snedjemib-Inti mention King Izezi himself being in the document office, noting that 'his person too would write with his own fingers'.[51] Likewise, in a letter copied at the entrance to the tomb of Rashepses—another of Izezi's viziers and also 'Overseer for Writing Documents'—the king enthusiastically declares that,

> My person has seen this quite ideal writing that you have had brought from the gathering of officials on this ideal day of delighting the mind of Izezi very truly with what he very truly wants. What my person has wanted more than anything at any time is to see this writing of yours.

His joyful sentiments seemingly do broadcast the enjoyment of the written word for its own sake and, whatever the culture of writing in Egypt might have been previously, within the historical record the reign of Izezi stands as a watershed in the relationship between the human race and the written word.

As will have become apparent by now, this was the moment in history when biographies following the model of Metjen's became typical in tomb-chapels, and their two common themes are service to king and community along with the inherent, elemental integrity of honesty and good conduct in dealing with others. In a tomb at Giza from the reign of Izezi, a community-leader named Seshemnefer (not the vizier of the same name) summarizes this ideal, declaring that 'every day I have spoken the truth that the God loves; the ideal of my being is speaking up for people before kings'—which itself reads like an aphorism from Ptahhatp.[52] Then, of course, these are Ptahhatp's values: a way founded on commitment, responsibility and a good name rather than worldly gain or celebrity happens to be exactly what we find in *The Teaching of Ptahhatp*. No doubt, we would be naive to suppose that every person in authority adhered to this ideal: an actual letter (rather than an inscribed copy) sent to the palace from an army commander named Meryranakht fumes at the suggestion that he may be at fault in an argument with Sabni, the community-leader of Elephantine; more particularly, he fumes at the suggestion that palace officials would rather broker a compromise between these two powerful men than establish right from wrong. As he says, 'better that an honest person be loved than one utterly crooked'— which once again reads like an aphorism from Ptahhatp.[53] Nevertheless, during the Fifth Dynasty, Egyptians in all parts of the nation and immi-grants from other lands increasingly sought to present themselves according to this ideal, and pharaonic cemeteries began to multiply away from the traditional royal burial grounds—from Aswan in the far south to the Mediterranean coast.

Ptahhatp at the palace

The festival processions and building projects of kings were the mean-ingful axis of the Old Kingdom officials' calendar. Of course, this is the point where our preconceptions about life in the ancient court are liable to break down. To take a single example, *The Teaching of Ptahhatp* takes place in the king's audience-room, perhaps bringing to a modern read-er's mind mighty wooden gates and all the trimmings. Certainly palaces existed; in fact, two belonging to Izezi himself are mentioned in letters inscribed in the tomb of Snedjemib-Inti. First, in a letter copied at the tomb's entrance, the king comments, 'My person has seen that document of yours you wrote to let it be known that you have done all the building ordered to be done for the palace "Loving Izezi", built for the royal estate.' For this the king rewards Snedjemib-Inti with a lake garden like Metjen's (see page 71). A second letter mentions the commission to construct a palace for Izezi's kingship festival within an enclosure measuring 1,440 square cubits (0.57 km² or 140 acres). That said, however, not a trace of an Old Kingdom palace is known to us in archaeology, and it is debatable perhaps whether there were any at all in the sense we may imagine—though imagination is a powerful urge. The only palaces represented in the art of royal pyramid enclosures are themselves elements within the pyramid enclosures or royal temples,[54] and were erected for use in festivals, such as the kingship festival Izezi once celebrated in Heliopolis and recorded in the inscription on an elegant alabaster jar now in the Louvre (plate XVII).[55] Accordingly, the 'palaces' built by Snedjemib-Inti might well have been short-lived structures rather than sumptuous residences, with principal areas consisting of mud-brick buildings on raised platforms and elsewhere perhaps not much more than tents pitched within a corral or stockade, like a perfunctory model of the Step Pyramid enclosure (see page 94). Certainly 'palaces' were built far from Saqqara and Giza, such as the palace built for King Huni of the Third Dynasty on Elephantine Island on the southern border of the country.[56] In royal letters of this period, the place to which officials return from their travels is often simply described as the 'Inside' or 'Interior' and is commensurate with wherever the king happens to be at that moment.

This should not surprise us, because the tomb biographies of his officials indicate that the king was characteristically travelling by boat in what a high priest of the time, Ptahshepses (see page 170), termed 'the gods' sailings in all the appearance festivals'—in other words, the public appearances of the king during religious festivals. As we noted already, nowadays we easily underestimate how much of life in the Old Kingdom was lived on the Nile, but the earliest images of Egyptian kings confirm as much. For example, an ebony label from the tomb of Aha, only the

CHAPTER 2

Ebony label from King Aha's tomb, with festival boats shown
in the third register. 10 cm (4 in.) wide. First Dynasty. Abydos.

second king of Egypt, shows the procession of boats sailing with the
king to named towns or communities—a procession known in his time
as 'following Horus'.[57] Above this scene, the king is shown making offerings in the temple at Hieraconpolis in the far south of the country, while
another temple or perhaps palace at Sais in the Nile Delta appears at the
very top.[58] A label from the burial of Qaʻa, the last king of the First Dynasty,
records the palace celebrating kingship festivals—just as Izezi would later
do—and accordingly building processional boats. On the Palermo Stone,
entries survive for three years in the reign of Snofru and record: (a) a
huge assault on Nubia, amassing 7,000 captives; (b) building thirty-five
enclosures in the desert to keep fighting bulls; and especially (c) the
ongoing, large-scale business of importing cedarwood and pinewood (?)
for 'making the gates of the king's palace' and building many and various
boats. These include two royal processional boats of a type named 'let
the Twin Lands adore' (i.e. the king in his public appearances)—each
measuring 100 cubits (52 metres or 170 feet), which is about 8.5 metres
(27½ feet) longer than the most famous of the wooden boats buried intact
beside the Great Pyramid of Khufu (plate xv).[59] Formally Snofru and
Izezi's festivals and their processional boats are descended directly from
those of Aha, Qaʻa and the earliest kings,[60] but then the earliest written

Ivory label for aromatic oils from the tomb of King Qaʻa, which records
a delivery of imported timber for a festival boat. First Dynasty. Abydos.

accounts flow directly out of prehistoric images of slender boats with high
prows and decorated cabins from the late fourth and early third millennium BC. Such drawings are not uncommon on promontories and steep
rock-faces in the principal wadis (seasonal river beds) that cut through
the surrounding desert and form highways to the Nile. Some of these
boats have dozens of rowers, others are pulled by ropes, but together they
also represent 'the gods' sailings in all the appearance festivals', much the
same as the river festivals in which Metjen first rowed out of obscurity.
At Giza, an inscription from the Fifth Dynasty tomb of Rawer relates a
remarkable incident that goes to the heart of the relationship between
king and official: 'The sovereign king Neferirkara made an appearance as
sovereign', it begins, 'on a day when the god's prow-rope gets taken.' In
other words, the king has arrived at a sacred site—perhaps even his own
pyramid enclosure—by boat and must now disembark, which, of course,
is among the most awkward manoeuvres anyone could face:

> Consequently the priest Rawer was at the feet of his person in his
> eminence as priest in order to manage the robes, when the staff that
> was in the grasp of his person struck the foot of the priest Rawer.
> Whereupon his person said, 'Are you alright?'

The crux of this incident is the king's concern for Rawer and, as a final note, the account of the incident 'was written beside the king himself at the palace's lake-entrance'.

Not only did the official life of the Old Kingdom often take place on boats but the imagery of this perpetual peregrination was transformed into the imagery of death and burial, not least insofar as the burials of kings were surrounded by the interments of multiple wooden boats. The royal companion Djadjamankh talks about reaching his tomb 'after crossing the lake' and 'after being ferried', while the tombs of Snedjemib-Inti and others show the official's limestone sarcophagus and lid being ferried from the quarry. By the end of the Fifth Dynasty funerary texts were inscribed inside royal tombs for the first time and the poetry of these chants or speeches entwines distinct but harmonious visions of the immortal and eternal, including the Creator's endless sailing through the firmament, forming the physical world out of potential (plate XVI):

> King Teti has taken his pure seat, which is in the sun's lead boat. Now the rowers who row the sun are the ones who are going to row Teti. The rowers who take the sun round the horizon are the ones who are going to row Teti round the horizon.[61]

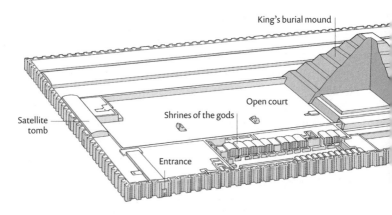

Standing 60 m (196½ ft) high, the Step Pyramid is the link between the earliest kings' tombs and the pyramids that follow. The complex embodies the form of a temple (see page 184), and may be our best model of an Old Kingdom palace (see page 91).

The same speeches picture Egypt coming together by boat for the king's funeral:

> The town of Pe is sailing upstream to you, and Hieraconpolis is sailing downstream to you. For you now the mourner is wailing, for you now the mortuary priest is robing.[62]

In fact, rowing the king in procession remained a formal aspect of the life of officials throughout the entire pharaonic period until 196 BC, when—as the celebrated Rosetta Stone records—many priests and other ruling officials finally refused to row King Ptolemy V as a member of a discredited regime, more than 2,000 years after Ptahhatp had explained the nature of success to King Izezi. So, as we read *The Teaching of Ptahhatp* we should not imagine Ptahhatp addressing Izezi in a towering stone hall: more likely they met in tents or boat cabins or in mud-brick rooms with posts made from twisted rushes and reeds, at various stops on the endless tour of the nation's innumerable shrines and festivals. There, as the high priest Ptahshepses explains, the king would let the vizier 'kiss his foot because his person does not make him kiss the ground'.

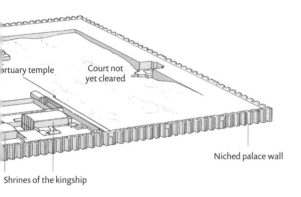

mortuary temple   Court not yet cleared

Niched palace wall

Shrines of the kingship

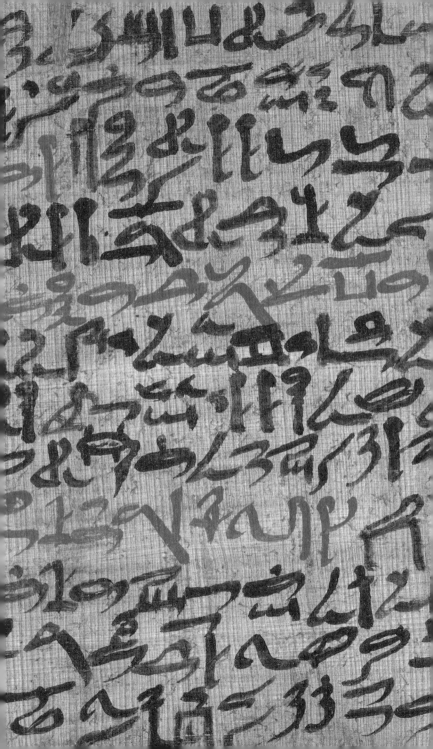

3

THE OLDEST BOOK IN THE WORLD

Listening or not listening is a choice and a
person's choice is life, prosperity and health to them.
A listener surely listens and speaks as such, but
a lover of listening is one who acts on what was said.

THE TEACHING OF PTAHHATP,
Second Conclusion

I. THE TEACHING OF PTAHHATP

Tʜɪs ᴛʀᴀɴsʟᴀᴛɪᴏɴ, including the division of the book into separate sections on the basis of rubrics (phrases written in red ink in
the original and here reproduced in **bold text**), follows the layout of
the hieratic text of P.Prisse as the only complete copy of *The Teaching
of Ptahhatp*. However, to be clear, the titles of the sections have been
added for the purpose of translation, are not present in the Egyptian
original, and there is probably little for the reader to lose by ignoring
them. Footnotes headed L1 and L2 indicate words, sentences or other
extra information provided by P.London 1 and P.London 2 respectively,
as the principal witnesses to alternative text traditions (see page 54).
That said, the Prologue and certain teachings have been translated twice
here—that is, following both the text of P.Prisse and an alternative text
—simply to avoid what would otherwise be excessive footnotes. In such
instances, the main text remains that of P.Prisse and the alternative
version is enclosed in a box.

Throughout the Teaching and those that follow afterwards, generic
Ancient Egyptian nouns and pronouns are often masculine in form (at
least, as we term such things in our modern grammatical terminology),
including 'he', 'a man' and so on. For the translation of P.Prisse, I have
rendered them into English using gender-neutral terms, such as 'they',
'a person'. However, the footnotes retain the original form of words
so that the original style is still apparent as you read. Using gender-
neutral terms for the teaching specifically about marriage (Twenty-first
Teaching) seems to me to render the translation unduly burdened with
paraphrases and at the same time disdain the original Egyptian cultural
context, whereas this is not the case for various teachings about personal
integrity by reference to sexual lust, sexual fidelity and paedophilia.

Insofar as there was no formal school system in pharaonic Egypt,
children's education took place within a family or a particular community. Accordingly, the Ancient Egyptian words 'father' (*yet*) and 'son'
(*sa'*) have been translated as 'teacher' and 'student' as and when the text

indicates an educational context but, for obvious reasons, not when a family context is clearly intended.

Another crucial word here is Ancient Egyptian *seru*, which is conventionally translated in Egyptology as 'officials' by analogy with a term used in Western systems of government. However, in *The Teaching of Ptahhatp* it refers to people who have been educated and act accordingly, as opposed to 'the ignorant', 'the careless', 'critics' and so on. As such, the translation 'responsible people', more in keeping with the sense of personal development and accountability, seems applicable. It also avoids making the translation seem unduly bureaucratic — a charge often levelled at this text, however unfairly.

Finally, note that Ptahhatp's use of the word 'God' (*netjer*) is discussed in some detail in Chapters 4 and 5.

*

The sequences in which the teachings appear in the principal manuscripts are as follows:

		teachings													
P.Prisse	o	1	2	3	4	5	6	7	8	9	10	11	12	13	14	15
P.London 1		*lost*													
P.London 2	o	1	2	3	4	5	6	7	8	9	10	11	12	13	14	

		teachings													
P.Prisse	o	16	17	18	19	20	21	22	23	24	25	26	27	28	29	30
P.London 1		*lost*		20	19	21	22	23	24	25	26	27	28	29	30
P.London 2	o	16	17	19	20	18	22	21	23	24	26	25	27	28	?	30

		teachings							conclusions							
P.Prisse	o	31	32	33	34	35	36	37	1	2	3	4	5	6	7	*
P.London 1		31	32	33	34	35	36	37	1	2	3	4	5	6	7	*
P.London 2	o	36?	?	30	33	34	35	37	*lost*		3		*lost*			

o prologue   * colophon

Prologue

p. 4 **The teaching of the Overseer of the City and Vizier Ptahhatp before** the person of the hereditary and sovereign king Izezi, who is living for all time until eternity.

The community-leader and vizier Ptahhatp says,

'O, benevolence, my lord, infirmity has happened, old age has arrived, tiredness has turned up and my frailty is building. Each day one spends the time distressed—my eyesight is reduced, my ears made deaf and my strength is failing because of mental fatigue.

'A silenced mouth cannot speak.

p. 5 'An empty mind cannot recall yesterday. Bones ache through their length, the very best has become bad, and every taste has left me. What old age does to people is wicked in every way. The nose is blocked and cannot breathe for the difficulty of standing and sitting.

'A disciple should be appointed for this humble servant so I may tell them words worth hearing, counsels from past times once heard by gods.

'So may the same be done for you. May sorrows be banished from the people, may both riverbanks be at work for you.'

So the person of this god says,

'Teach them, then, the historic words that they may go on to act as a model for the children of responsible people, who may be educated to listen to every bit of information told to them. No one will be born wise.'

P. LONDON 2

Beginning of the teaching from the elite-member, community-leader, god's father, god's beloved, judge in the six great temples, a voice to bring harmony throughout the land, Overseer of the City and Vizier Ptahhatp, as he speaks before the person of the hereditary and sovereign king Izezi.

'Infirmity has happened, old age has arrived, the body is growing tired, only the old days are real, and my strength is failing because I am mentally fatigued. A silenced mouth cannot speak, my eyesight is reduced and ears made deaf. Each day my mind spends its time in tears. An empty mind cannot recall yesterday. Bones ache from growing old.

'**The nose is blocked and cannot breathe**, standing and sitting are painful, the very best has become bad, and every taste has left. What old age does to people is wicked in every way.

'Have a disciple appointed for this humble servant so my student may stand in my place and I may teach them words worth hearing.

'**Counsels from past times**[1] that once served the ancestors, may they do the same for you. May sorrows be banished from the people, may both riverbanks be at work for you.'

So the person of this god says,

'Then, since you are seated here, teach them the historic words and make them a model for the children of responsible people, who may be educated to listen to every bit of information told to them. No one will be born wise.'

1 Written above the line.

First Teaching. On learning

Beginning of the phrases of speaking the ideal spoken by the elite-member, community-leader, god's father, god's beloved, king's eldest son of his body, Overseer of the City and Vizier Ptahhatp, in teaching the uneducated to know and be the definition of speaking the ideal—transformative for whoever will listen, hobbling whoever tries to step over it.

So he would speak before his son.[1]

Do not be high-minded because you are educated.[2] Rather, consult with the simple as much as the educated. The limits of no art can be attained—no artist is equipped with their fulfilment.[3]

Wise words are rarer than malachite yet found among the girls at the grindstones.

1 L2 'so he spoke before his son, little Ptahhatp' as a rubric.
2 L2 adds 'do not be satisfied because you are educated'.
3 L2 has a red X above the line here and the phrase is completed at the foot of the page.

Second Teaching. On argument

If you meet someone looking for an argument—a stubborn person, cleverer than you—reach out your hand and bow politely. Just as you disagree with them, they are not going to agree with you.

Make little of nonsense by not getting into an argument with them. Let it be said of them that that one's a fool, and let your self-restraint match their advantages.[1]

1 L2 'that one's a fool, and so do not end up more angry than they are worth'.

Third Teaching. On argument

If you meet someone looking for an argument[1]—an equal who is on your level—show that you are better than them with silence.

While they are talking their nonsense, the chatter among critics will be great, while your reputation remains as exemplary as responsible people knew it to be already.[2]

1 L2 writes this phrase as a rubric, as we may anticipate, though P. Prisse does not.
2 L2 'the chatter among critics may be respectful but your reputation is still exemplary because responsible people have been entirely transformed'.

p. 6 ## Fourth Teaching. On argument

If you meet someone looking for an argument—someone ordinary, not your equal—do not abuse them precisely because they are not up to the task: let them have the floor and they will defeat themself.

Do not talk back to them to amuse yourself. Do not laugh at someone who has come to you.[1]

Humiliating the hapless is perverse, and you are going to get what you want anyway.[2] You should get the better of them by using the self-discipline of responsible people.

1 L2 'who is your opponent'.
2 L2 'is perverse and he is just going to do what he wants'.

Fifth Teaching. On truth

Whenever you are in charge, accountable for the circumstances of many, seek the meaning for you in every event until your conduct becomes impeccable. Truth is ever important,[1] ever relevant. It has not been changed since the beginning of time.[2]

Anyone who oversteps principles meets with consequences, which is what the greedy[3] overlook. Pettiness is what grabs at excess but crookedness has never established itself as the standard.[4] Whoever says 'I have got myself caught' never admits that 'I got caught because of my own choices'.

The definition of truth shall be that it is constant and people cannot say that it is only for their teacher.

1 L2 'truth is transformative'.
2 Literally 'since the time of Osiris' (see page 150).
3 L2 'the uneducated'.
4 Literally 'moored its own example.'

Sixth Teaching. On fear

You should not create fear among people, God responds accordingly.

When someone says 'I can live by it (fear)', apparently they believe they can do without food.

When someone says 'I am powerful', they are saying 'I am trapped in my self-importance'.

When someone says they will strike another, they end up given over to what they cannot control.[1]

Because what people fear has never yet happened—only what God requires happens. So, resolve to live happily and whatever is given will come of its own accord.

1 L2 makes this phrase a rubric.

Seventh Teaching. On company

Whenever you are sitting to dine with someone more important than you, take what is politely offered to you.[1] When you look at what is in front of you do not eye it up

p. 7   with greedy glances. Grabbing is a spiritual offence.

Do not speak to them until they ask a question because how do you know what they do not like to hear? Speak only when they address you and what you say is bound to be what is wanted.[2]

Whenever someone important is entertaining,[3] business is conducted as their spirit dictates and they are going to give to whomever they favour. When the night's business happens, it is the spirit that reaches out its arms. Someone important may give but no one just gets.

How much we get is based on God's plan[4] and only the uneducated complain about this.

1   L2 adds 'Do not stare at whoever is in their company'.
2   L2 adds 'Keep looking down until he addresses you, speak when he addresses you, laugh only after he laughs, and you are ideal in his opinion indeed. What you do is bound to be what is wanted, though what is wanted cannot be known.'
3   In L2 this is a rubric.
4   Literally 'eating bread is based on God's plan'.

Eighth Teaching. On being scrupulous

Whenever you are trusted to convey information and sent from someone important to someone else important, do exactly as they sent you to do. Conduct another's business for them just as they ask.[1]

Resist the urge! Do not twist any words because you are involving someone important with someone else important. Stick to the facts,[2] without introducing the point of view of another's opinions— important or trivial, it is a spiritual offence.

1   L2 'just as he says, swallowing your own point of view about what was said to you, guarding against any possible negligent thought.'
2   Literally 'observe the truth through its likeness'. In L2 this is a rubric.

Ninth Teaching. On success

If you cultivate flowers in the marshes, God has done great things through you.[1] Do not talk yourself up[2] with those close to you— keeping a respectful silence is better.[3] When a possessor of wealth possesses integrity, they seize goodwill[4] like a crocodile seizes.

Do not demean someone who has no children, do not belittle them by boasting about the matter. A father may end up great with grief. And a mother who has just given birth—nonetheless, another may still be happier than her.

God alone looks after the lonely, while the employer of a whole workforce may pray to only have to follow.

1   L2 'God has made it great for you'.
2   Literally 'puff up your comments'.
3   L2 'you should not be full of boasting, do not scorn the poor, and watch your comments beside your neighbours—showing some respect by silence would be better'.
4   Literally 'from the community'.

Tenth Teaching. On humility

If you are not up to a task, follow someone smarter[1] and your prospects are immaculate before God.

As you knew only ordinary people previously, you should not now be smug toward anybody just because you know what they used to be. Respect them for what they have achieved.

Surely nothing has come from itself—that is a principle specifically for those who love themselves. As far as bettering themselves goes, they did so[2] but it was God who made their talent and God coaches them while they sleep.

1 L2 'if you are inadequate, you should follow a smart person'.
2 L2 'as for bettering oneself, it should be respected'.

Eleventh Teaching. On quiet resolution

Trust your mind[1] all the time of your being. Do not add to what has already been said.[2] Never go against your mind.[3] Doing so is a spiritual offence.[4]

Do not spend one moment of the day except in strengthening the foundation of your home. As you gain possessions, trust your mind— there is no real gain when it grows dull.

1 L2 'trust your spirit'.
2 L2 'do not add to your speaking'.
3 Literally 'do not reduce any of the time of trusting your mind'.
4 Literally 'cutting its time is a spiritual offence'.

Twelfth Teaching. On bringing up children

As you are a smart person you should raise a child to please God.

If they are decent, follow your example and support you in your affairs,[1] do the very best for them. This is your child, who belongs to the outpouring of your spirit. You should not take them for granted.

Of course, seed may create a rival. If they go astray, go against your advice, turn against all you say and their comments turn into useless words, punish them as necessary for their comments.

Whoever attacks you is one who is condemned.

p. 8 The fact is that their attitude was determined in the womb because those who will be guided do not go wrong, whereas those who are stranded do not seek a ferry.

1 Literally 'his behaviour binds your belongings to their rightful place'.

P. LONDON 2

If you are a capable person and your home has been made ready, you should raise a child to please God.

If they are decent, follow your example, listen to your teaching, their conduct is a benefit in your home and they support you in your affairs,[1] look to make every moment the best for them. This is your child, who your spirit pours out for you. You should not take them for granted.

Of course, seed may create a rival. If they go astray and go against your advice, then they will not act out your teaching, their conduct will be useless in your home, they will turn against all you say, and their comments will stray into useless words that have gone beyond what they have seen so they are no longer in control of them.

You should send them away because they are not your child. They were not born to you. Punish them as appropriate for their attitude. That one of them is one who is condemned. The fact is that God took away their difficulties[2] in the womb so those who will be guided do not go wrong, whereas those who are stranded do not seek a ferry.

1 Literally 'his behaviour binds your belongings to their rightful place'.
2 In a funerary context at least, this phrase (*hu sedjbu*) certainly means 'overcome difficulties'.

Thirteenth Teaching. On humility

Whenever you are in the audience-room,[1] **stand and sit** at the appropriate moments.[2] The very first day has been arranged for you.

Do not simply walk in and get yourself barred as a consequence.[3] One whose entrance is properly announced is well regarded, and comfortable is the situation of whoever was invited. The audience-room is set at the standard, all its conduct measured from plumb. Only God advances a situation,[4] so the pushy have not made it this far.

1 In other words, where the king receives visitors from outside the palace. The reference in pharaonic terms to a standard of behaviour fixed in the presence of the king since the beginning of time is crucial (see page 135), so compare also the Epilogue for *The Teaching of Kagemni* below.
2 Literally 'at your steps'.
3 L2 'do not sneak in late in case you get thrown out'.
4 L2 'only God makes excellence and advances the situation of fresh faces'.

Fourteenth Teaching. On indulgence

Whenever you are with people, keep company with those who veil their thoughts and veil [your own] thoughts. One who does not let talking pour out of their belly gains self-control. Those who gain other things have given what as their advice?

As your reputation is immaculate, you need not speak; but your body gets fattened by you even more than by those close to you, and you get puffed up from what you do not even realize.

There is a thought that listens to its appetite and puts its wants where its needs should be, and so its mind gets wasted and its body reduced.

Great are the thoughts given by God but whoever listens to their appetite belongs to an enemy.

P. LONDON 2

Whenever you are with people, keep company with those who veil their thoughts. Veiling your own thoughts is best for your reputation as one who does not listen to what his appetite says, while one who has possessions is what? Whoever knows this and so gains self-control, they have respect in keeping with their dignity. Those with possessions have only possessions.

As your reputation is immaculate, you need not speak; but your body gets fattened by you even more than by those close to you, and you get puffed up from what you do not even realize.

A thought that listens to its appetite goes astray and puts its wants where its needs should be. As a consequence its mind gets wasted and its body reduced because the thought is self-defeating.

A thought burns because it is God-given but whoever listens to their own desires belongs to an enemy.

Fifteenth Teaching. On pretence[1]

Report your affairs without hesitation, offer your advice in your employer's office.

If a promotion comes on the back of something someone has demonstrated, there can be nothing uncomfortable about then being summoned to give a report. There is no humiliation lying in wait in the question 'Who is it, again, who knows about this stuff?' Whoever makes themselves out to be more important than their actual achievements is the one who gets embarrassed.

If anyone would rather show discipline, they stop speaking at 'I have said my piece.'

1 This teaching is only known from P. Prisse.

Sixteenth Teaching. On humility

Whenever you are in charge,

p. 9 wide-ranging through the affairs entrusted to you, do things so appropriate that the days to come will remember them.[1]

Clarity can never come about amid praise.[2] The thinly veiled disgust that actually happens is disdain.

1 L2 'give appropriate advice, mindful of the days to come'.
2 L2 'a good example cannot happen amid praise'.

I Preparing papyrus. An unkempt man brings cut stems from the marsh, while a well-groomed official strips off the rind. Tomb of Puyemra. Eighteenth Dynasty, reign of Thutmose III. West Thebes.

II The Thirty-third and Thirty-fourth Teachings of Ptahhatp in Papyrus London 1. This copy is written in vertical columns, in the archaic style, and without red ink. 13.5 cm (5¼ in.) high. Late Middle Kingdom. Provenance uncertain, probably West Thebes.

111 Tomb-chapel of Metjen. His biography decorates the entrance passage but the near (southern) wall has been removed for display. Limestone. 2.52 m (8 ft 3¼ in.) high. Fourth Dynasty, reign of Snofru. Saqqara.

IV The Step Pyramid complex of Netjerkhet Djoser (see pages 92–93) exemplifies the standard layout of the earliest pharaonic temples (see page 184). Third Dynasty. Saqqara.

V Statue of Metjen from the serdab of his tomb chapel. Granite. 47 cm (1 ft 6½ in.) high. Fourth Dynasty, reign of Snofru. Saqqara.

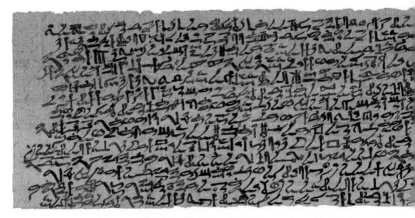

VI Beginning of *The Teaching of Ptahhatp* in Papyrus Prisse. 15 cm (6 in.) high. Late Middle Kingdom. West Thebes.

VII Prologue and the First Teaching in Papyrus London 2. 30 cm (11¾ in.) high. Eighteenth Dynasty. Probably West Thebes.

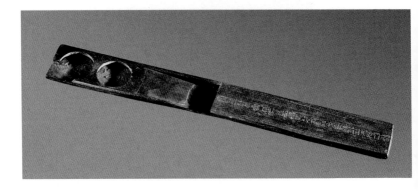

VIII Wooden writing case (*gesti*) with hollows for cakes of powdered black and red ink (*ryt*), and a slot for reed pens (*'awr*). 41 cm (1 ft 4 in.) long. Late Old Kingdom. Provenance unknown.

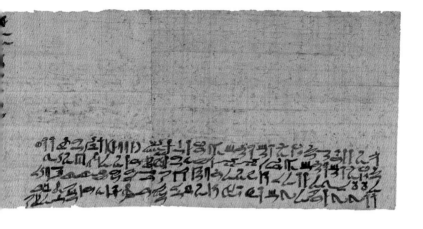

IX Statue of an anonymous prince, illustrating the ordinary pose for writing (see page 46). Painted limestone. 54 cm (1 ft 9¼ in.) high. Fourth or Fifth Dynasty. Saqqara.

x Partially reconstructed entrance to the ruinous tomb of Vizier Ptahhatp I.
Fifth Dynasty, reign of Izezi. Saqqara.

XI Izezi's vizier, Ptahhatp (scenes in the tomb of Ptahhatp II copied from the tomb of Ptahhatp I).
The vizier seated at the table with food for his *ka* or immortal 'presence' (see page 84).
On the left, he inhales perfume made for a kingship festival, from an alabaster jar (see plate XVII).

XII Staff in hand, the vizier supervises the activity on his own funerary estate
(see pages 71–73, and 136–39). On the left, his son Akhethatp stands by his feet; on the right,
he is with his eldest son, Ptahhatp. Fifth Dynasty. Saqqara.

XIII Life-size statue of Vizier Ptahhatp I, wearing a fashionable wig and goatee, presumably from a serdab in his tomb-chapel. Plastered wood. Fifth Dynasty, reign of Izezi. Saqqara.

XIV Statue of a king's son and the Overseer of All the King's Building, Hemiunu. Painted limestone. 1.55 m (5 ft 1 in.) high. Fourth Dynasty. Giza.

xv King Khufu's boat. Since prehistory river boats had been the centrepiece of Egyptian festivals. Cedar wood. 43.5 m (142 ft 8½ in.) long. Fourth Dynasty. Giza.

XVI The 'Big Bang' of writing. Izezi's successor, Wenis, lay in a sarcophagus enclosed by walls decorated as though a tent beneath the stars, while for the first time hieroglyphs erupt through a royal tomb like computer code (see pages 94–95). Fifth Dynasty. Saqqara.

XVII Jar inscribed for the first kingship festival of Izezi. Alabaster. 16.3 cm (6½ in.) high. Fifth Dynasty.

XVIII King Khufu, subject of one of the oldest surviving books (see page 57). Ivory. 7.5 cm (3 in.) high. Date uncertain. Abydos.

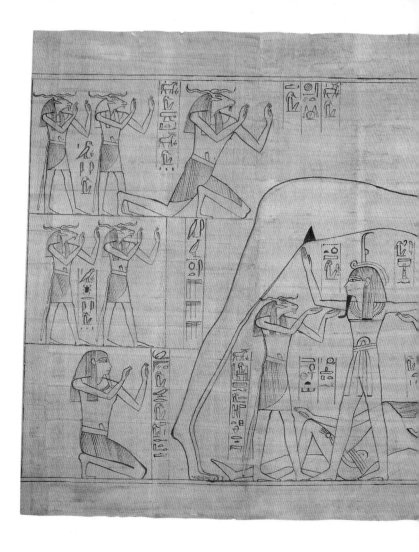

XIX The shape of creation, from the funerary scroll (or 'Book of the Dead')
of a high-born lady, Nesitanebtashru. Our world is a bubble in unbounded potential.
Reaching out, Light (Shu) forms the vault of Nut (said to bring the sun to the sky)
above the supine mass of Geb (said to bring the sun to this world). At bottom right,
the deceased emerges from her tomb into the far side of the sky, where the
souls of the gods, of the dead and of those to come, mass in adoration.
47 cm (1 ft 6½ in.) high. Tenth century BC. West Thebes.

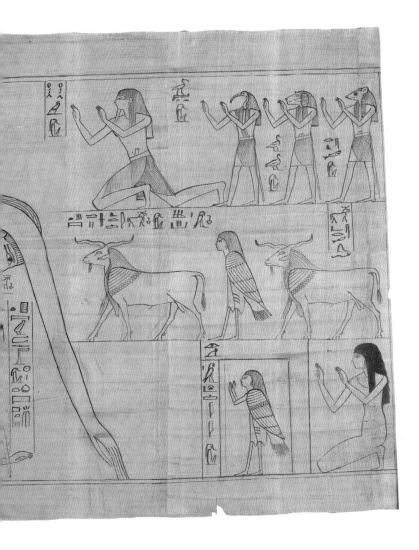

xx Today little can be seen of the temple of Ptah in Memphis, but it was probably the largest in the world for many centuries. Its ancient name may even be the origin of our word 'Egypt' (see page 170). The water table visible among the ruins recalls how even the land in Egypt is formed by the Nile.

xxi The Shabaka Stone. Obvious damage from later reuse divides the hieroglyphic text into two sections, with *Why Things Happen* fully preserved on the right. Breccia. 1.37 m (4 ft 6 in.) wide. Twenty-fifth Dynasty. Alexandria.

xxii View of Shabaka's pyramid complex, now much reduced, in the royal cemetery at al-Kurru, Sudan. Twenty-fifth Dynasty.

XXIII Egyptian stela recording a land donation in the Nile Delta during the reign of Shabaka, shown top right. Limestone. 37.5 cm (1 ft 2¾ in.) high. Twenty-fifth Dynasty. Provenance unknown, probably Desouk.

Seventeenth Teaching. On listening

Whenever you are in charge, you should enjoy listening to whoever comes to you with questions. Do not interrupt them until they have emptied their belly of what they wanted to say.[1]

Those who rely on you need to say what is on their mind even more than they need to get something done about it.[2]

When a request simply gets refused, people wonder why would it come to that? Not everything people ask you for can happen but the purpose of listening is to clear the air.

1 L2 'until he says what he came to say'.
2 L2 'anyone with a request wants someone to take his demands seriously more than he wants what he came for done. He is happier than anyone who ever had a request granted about any matter listened to in the past. Ideal listening is clearing the air'.

Eighteenth Teaching. On lust

If you wish to maintain friendships within a home you come into as an employer, a family member or a friend—or any other place you enter—resist the urge! Keep away from the opposite sex.

Any place this goes on cannot be as it should be. Eyes cannot see clearly—a thousand people would lose sight of what is good for them.[1]

The mere moment seems to be a dream but you can go to your grave still thinking about it.[2] It is a worthless gamble provoked by an enemy[3] but the thought comes up and the mind forgets itself.[4]

As for one lost in lusting so, their prospects cannot flourish.

1 L2 instead 'you are bedazzled by sparkling skin and stand there turned to carnelian'.
2 L2 instead 'the outcome brings death before that great saying gets appreciated: "Do not demean <your> character <in the way> that men do a thousand things not worth doing"'.
3 Literally 'a worthless suggestion fired by an enemy'.
4 L2 adds 'do not do it, it is a deceit and you will lose the benefit of each day'.

Nineteenth Teaching. On greed[1]

If you wish your conduct to be exemplary and

p. 10 remove yourself from any misconduct, resist any opportunity for greed.

It is a sick infestation[2] for which there is no cure. It infects fathers and mothers, brothers from the same mother.[3] It alienates wife and husband. It is a compound of every evil, a bundle of everything detestable.

A person gets through life by observing truth and walking a step at a time. This way they fashion a legacy but the greedy leave no leftovers behind.

1 The surviving text of P.London 1 picks up at this point.
2 Literally 'infection of worms'.
3 L1 and L2 add 'it embitters a sweet friend, it distances a trusted employee from his employer'.

Twentieth Teaching. On greed

Do not be greedy in sharing. Do not covet even your own slice.

Do not be greedy even with those close to you.[1] The claim of the humble is greater than that of the mighty and whoever lets down those close to them is contemptible—deprived of the right to speak.

Just a slice of what you desire so much makes a rival out of the calmest belly.

1 L2 'do not do what you want with those close to you'.

Twenty-first Teaching. On marriage

If you are smart and look after your home, you should love your wife the correct way. Fill her belly and clothe her back.[1] Perfume is a pleasure for her body. Make her glad of all the time that she has you. She is a field that transforms the one who has her.

You should not make her choose between things that matter to her—keep away from her the kind of control that constrains her. Her eye may be full of fury when she realizes.[2] This is about keeping her in your home, about you retaining her devotion. Whatever she had hoped to get, once she has it all around, so her devotion will flow.[3]

1 L2 'fill her belly and oil her skin'.
2 L1 and L2 add 'clear the air with her about whatever you might have done'.
3 Literally 'a canal has been made for her' but note that the Ancient Egyptian word for 'canal' (*mer*) sounds the same as the verb 'love', while the word for 'devotion' is actually the word 'fluid' (*mu*) used in the original sense of English 'humour'. L1 reads 'a woman to whom things have been given, once she has it all around, <a canal> has been made for her'.

p. 11 **Twenty-second Teaching. On friendship**

Gladden your trusted friends with what you have gained.
This has happened because of God's favour. What do they say about whoever fails to look after their trusted friends? 'This one is an acquisitive spirit, but when they look to tomorrow what happens cannot be known.'[1]

The spirit that brings gladness with it is the correct spirit. Whenever celebrations happen, trusted friends are the ones who say 'Come in!'

Gladness does not come with home delivery:[2] when it is not there, trusted friends have to come over.[3]

1 L1 and L2 have here 'there is no knowing his affairs when he plans for tomorrow'.
2 Literally 'cannot be fetched to the quay'.
3 L2 'when it is lacking it comes with trusted friends'.

Twenty-third Teaching. On gossip

You should not repeat gossip from someone who did not actually hear the matter. It stems from jealousy.[1]

Repeat only statements of fact[2] rather than listening to a world of piss-taking. No, genuine understanding is there before your eyes.

When a theft gets ordered to be done, the one who does the thieving is the one sentenced in law.

No, this is ruination from fantasy — look the other way.[3]

1 L1 adds 'Speak the matter <without repeating from> one who has not heard. You should be your own basis, without needing gossip.'
2 Literally 'statements of the seen'.
3 L1 'a lie is like the moment in a dream that ruins it. Keep away from it.'

Twenty-fourth Teaching. On when to speak

Whenever you are a smart person, sitting in their employer's office, inspire every mind to excellence.[1]

Your silence is more effective than guessing.[2] You should say only what you know how to explain. The office wordsmith makes speaking more clumsy than any job. The one who can explain is the only one who can make the point.

1 L1 and L2 add 'choose your comments and inspire'.
2 L1 'Silence is more effective for you than what you make up.'

Twenty-fifth Teaching. On quiet leadership

When you hold power create respect by knowing your business
and by speaking calmly. Do not give an order that is not appropriate.
Confrontation brings in conflict.

p. 12   Do not be haughty or you may get taken down. Do not be silent just
to walk in secret.

Answer an accusation but take the long view and leave yourself
options. A hothead's steam drifts all over but composure lays
out its path.

Whoever worries all day will not inspire one positive moment.
Whoever hides away all day will not build leadership.[1]

In the end, someone who gambles is just the same as the most
carefully prepared—if an opportunity falls flat and someone else
grabs it, the mind thinks 'If only!'

1   Literally 'establish the estate for himself'.

Twenty-sixth Teaching. On loyalty

Do not push yourself to the fore[1] when someone becomes important. Do not resent the one who bears the burden nor give them cause to resent you for challenging them.[2]

A spirit may relax with whoever loves it—it is about spirits giving along with God. What a spirit wants is that something is done for it, and so you will be well regarded again, even after a fit of temper.

As much as there is contentment in the presence of such a spirit, there is only opposition in the presence of enemies.[3] This is about spirits nurturing love.[4]

1   L1 'Do not praise yourself when someone becomes important'.
2   L1 'Do not resent the one who bears the burden: set it (the burden) on the ground, a rest for his spirit. When difficulties befall and challenge him, then you will be well regarded again, even after a fit of temper'.
3   L1 'your spirit' and 'your enemies'.
4   L1 'what gives love is the spirit'. Note that the Ancient Egyptian word 'spirits' (ka'u) sounds the same as the word for 'nourishment'.

Twenty-seventh Teaching. On loyalty

Teach an important person what transforms them. Arrange it so they get this (education) and people can notice. You should let their own innate wisdom come out of them,[1] and in the presence of their spirit there is benefit for you too.[2] A bellyful of love is more than satisfying—it puts clothes on your back.

Let them take notice of you and so your own situation can reach your own expectations.[3] There is still a living to make on this basis and, of course, they do take care of you.[4] Still, should they make even the finest gesture for you, keep quiet. You see, for the love of you to endure it must do so in the bellies of those who really do love you.

What wants to listen is the spirit.[5]

1 L1 'let your wisdom come down and complete him'.
2 L1 instead 'it should be received as compassion requires, and on that basis you are immaculate'.
3 Literally 'in order that your estate may do well in terms of the responsibilities you would want'.
4 L1 'on that basis, and you will make the finest co-worker when you are at the loom'.
5 L1 'what listening wants is what your spirit wants'.

p. 13 ## Twenty-eighth Teaching. On integrity

If you produce a student sufficiently high-born for public office, a representative[1] for what matters to lots of people, cut your ties scrupulously.[2]

You must speak and not take sides. Take care that the student too can speak their own opinions, and also that responsible people let them talk on behalf of those they represent or you may simply end up as an example of a conflict of interest.

1 L1 'someone responsible'.
2 L1 '... ... judging with partiality <between> two people. Bias disgusts God ... ...'.

Twenty-ninth Teaching. On integrity

If you are compassionate in the moment that has happened, you will acknowledge a person for their honesty and leave them be.[1]

Do not single someone out because they have never once paid you any attention.[2]

1   L1 'incline towards a man for his need and leave him alone'.
2   Literally 'do not remember him because he has been silent to you since the first day.' L1 adds 'As for punishment without a crime, it is how a criminal goes about treating someone.'

Thirtieth Teaching. On humility

If you become great when once you were ordinary—perhaps you became wealthy after previously being poor in the community you know—do not rewrite your own history.[1] Do not misrepresent your success, which has happened for you out of God's gifts.

Do you not stand in a line behind someone else just like you, for whom the same things have already happened?

1   Literally 'do not second-guess what happened to you previously'.

Thirty-first Teaching. On integrity

Defer to your boss, who stands above you in the greater scheme of things,[1] and your career is soundly based on achievements[2] and your benefits are in their proper place.

Whoever argues with their boss is a nuisance but you do well only as long as they are sympathetic. It does not hurt to roll up your sleeves.

Do not steal the work of colleagues.

p. 14   Do not plagiarize the work of someone who collaborates with you.[3] Do not oblige them to go on at you before you will listen to them. They may be a stupid shrew but, even if they are known to be a troublemaker, it is humiliating to have to argue your business in public.[4]

1 Literally 'your overseer from the king's estate'. L1 'your overseer from the audience-room'.
2 L1 'on excellence'.
3 L1 adds 'this is not how to transform them'.
4 Literally 'in any responsibility to get approached'. L1 'it is humiliating to argue with someone who comes at you'.

Thirty-second Teaching. On lust

You should not have sex with a juvenile. With the immature[1] you know what is condemned: 'There is no satisfying what is in such an appetite and they should not risk doing what is condemned.[2] They will be at peace only after they extinguish their desires.'

1 Literally 'the fluid-at-heart'.
2 L1 adds 'he will not be quiet'.

Thirty-third Teaching. On getting to know others

If you want to find out about your colleague's character, do not
ask around, go to them. Take a moment with them alone until you
are no longer unsure on the matter. Question them after a time.
Ask their opinions when there is a moment to talk.

If their past experience comes out of them—they do things that
make you indisposed to them or even to being friendly at all—
do not be haughty, be measured.

Take care not to let them know your opinion.[1] Do not respond with
an excuse for rudeness. Do not resent them. Do not humiliate them.[2]

What will be will be.[3] There is no escaping what is in store for us.[4]

1 Literally 'what you are saying'. L1 'in case you reveal to him what you are thinking'.
2 L1 adds something here but the reading is now lost.
3 Literally 'his end has never not come'.
4 Literally 'no one can escape what is fated for him'.

Thirty-fourth Teaching. On sharing

Smile all the time of your being. Whatever has left the store
cannot go back in.

Only bread meant for sharing

p. 15 provokes resentment—an accuser has an empty belly. An accuser
comes out of need—do not give anyone cause to come after you,
when there can be the joy of remembering a person years after they
have left us.

Thirty-fifth Teaching. On integrity

Know your plumage when wealth is yours. Do not be miserly to your friends.

'They are a field ripe for harvesting. They are greater than one's riches, and the wealth of each other.'[1]

The character of a person's student transforms them too. True integrity gets passed on.

1 Compare this use of an aphorism with the language of *The Teaching of Hordedef* below.

Thirty-sixth Teaching. On restraint

Discipline from the head, educate from the character. The restraint of force is going to bring out the real character. Any instance (of force) other than against an offence only causes someone, even in the wrong, to resent you.

Thirty-seventh Teaching. On tolerance

If you marry a cheat,[1] shameless and known to the town — duplicitous, prefers the time spent apart — do not throw them out.[2] Shamelessness tests your equanimity.

1 This word (*šepnet*) is unknown so the meaning is determined from the context. Reading *pešnet* '(someone) uncommitted' would seem desirable but *šepnet* is confirmed by the hieratic texts of P.Prisse and L2. Possibly *šepnet* is related to another word (*šep*) meaning 'blind'.
2 Literally 'let her eat'. L1 and L2 add 'though she is laughing with disdain, it may be said that'. The surviving text of L2 effectively ends at this point.

SEVEN CONCLUSIONS
First Conclusion. Become an example

If you listen to the things I have said to you, so all your prospects will improve.[1] Their demonstration of truth is their value. Recollection of them trips from people's mouths because of the perfection of their phrasing. Every sentence has been tested and has not failed on this earth in all of time.[2]

Devising a saying is to make the speaking of responsible people so much the better. It is teaching someone to speak to whoever comes later so they may listen and become a skilled listener. Speaking to whoever comes later is the ideal because only they can hear.

If an instance of the ideal happens through one who is in charge, they are meaningful for eternity. All their wisdom is for all of time. The educated person is the one who nurtures their soul by realizing on earth the ideal self within. The educated person is wise because of what they have learned.

The responsible person in their ideal moment through the action of their intention and of their tongue —

p. 16 whose lips are precise when speaking and their eyes in seeing, their ears accurate in hearing what is transformative for their student — is one who acts out truth free from error.[3]

1 L1 'all your prospects are like those <of former times>'.
2 L1 'has been tested and, because of the perfection of the phrasing, you shall endure on this earth <for all time>'.
3 See pages 186–9.

Second Conclusion. Learn to listen

Listening transforms a student who listens,[1] and listening comes from a listener. A listener comes from someone having listened.

Ideal is the listening and ideal the speaking of all who have heard what transforms.[2] Listening transforms the listener.

Listening is an ideal beyond anything—love of the ideal may happen. What could be better than a student learning as their teacher speaks? They shall grow old and still have this.

Listening is what God wants, and one who does not listen hates God. Listening or not listening is a choice[3] and a person's choice is life, prosperity and health to them. A listener surely listens and speaks as such, but a lover of listening is one who acts on what was said.

What could be better than a student listening to their teacher? How lucky the one who was told this, since a student who learns to listen is so attractive. Whoever listens and learns makes sense from deep within and is long remembered along with their teacher.[4] They are recalled in the comments of the living—those on earth now and those who are going to be.

1 L1 'listening to a listener transforms'.
2 L1 'ideal is the listening and ideal the discernment in speaking of whoever learns from someone who has caused listening <to what transforms>, and whoever wishes listening … …'.
3 Literally 'the intention is what causes its owner to be a listener or one who does not listen'. L1 clearly has a different text at this point but it is too broken to read.
4 Literally 'attains a funerary cult'.

Third Conclusion. Listening is a firm footing

If a high-born student[1] still learns when their teacher speaks, their prospects cannot go wrong. You should teach your student to be a listener

p. 17 who will excel among responsible people, whose comments will promote what they learned, who will have observed as a listener, and the student will make excellent progress past each error that one who does not listen is bound to have caused.

Teach the educated to give them a sure footing while the careless get stuck.[2]

1 Literally 'the child of a man'. L2 preserves a fragment of this conclusion.
2 Here L1 adds its version of the passage that appears at the end of the Fifth Conclusion in P. Prisse: 'Do not remove a single saying, do not add one. Its due place is what you should want. Resist the urge! Trust your instincts. Beware the know-it-all saying …'. The rest is lost.

Fourth Conclusion. Ignorance is self-defeating

As for the careless person who does not listen, there is nothing to be done for them.

Let them view learning as ignorance and what transforms as harm. Each day, instead of what would raise them they do everything demeaning. They live on what kills us, and what they consume is morbid. Stating their character[1] as such is simply what responsible people already know, and they say 'Life is dying every day'.

Their examples[2] will be ignored simply because of the number of mistakes reckoned against them each day.

1 L1 clearly has a different text at this point but it is too broken to read.
2 Literally 'his moments'.

Fifth Conclusion. Teach by example

A student who listens to what has been passed down through the ages[1] has the ideal. After listening they shall grow old and long be remembered.[2]

They shall pass on the same things to their children by living out their teacher's teaching. Every person, who is a teacher by the way they act, passes on as much to the next generation. This is how they inform their children.[3]

Show character,

p. 18   do not pass on your flaws.[4] Let truth be apparent so that the next generation may thrive. Whenever the first of a bunch has come with lies, then people who are watching later remark 'They are just the same as that first one,' and afterwards say to anyone who will listen 'They are just the same as that first one.'

They (the sayings) are things anyone can see and many will be thankful.[5] There are no real riches without knowing them. Do not remove a single saying, do not add one, do not put one in place of another. Resist the urge! Trust your instincts.[6] Beware the know-it-all saying, 'Listen to this instead, if you want to be popular in the comments of critics.'

You should speak as you have learned, following the example of the artist,[7] and speak openly about the exact moment when all your affairs came to be as they should be.

1 Literally 'as a follower of Horus' (see page 150). L1 'as a follower of God'.
2 Literally 'grow old and attain a funerary cult'.
3 P.Prisse is mistaken here ('in this way shall their children tell them') but L1 gives the correct reading.
4 In L1 the text of this conclusion is lost after this point. However, the final passage here, as it appears in P.Prisse, appears instead at the end of the Third Conclusion in L1 (see page 127).
5 The reference is to the conduct of people and how it may or may not reflect the teachings.
6 Literally 'do not undo the cords on you'.
7 See the Prologue.

Sixth Conclusion. Actions not words

When your mind is overflowing, restrain your mouth.
Then your conduct, even compared to responsible people, is
exemplary before your employer.

Act so that they get told 'That one is a proper student'

p. 19 and anyone else who hears gets told 'The one they were born
to is so lucky.'

Take your time when it is your turn to speak and you will say
appropriate things. Then responsible people are going to hear
and say 'What comes out of their mouth is simply immaculate.'

Seventh Conclusion. Live out your teaching

Act until your employer says about you 'This one is the finest their
teacher ever taught. They are cut from the same cloth[1] and they knew
it all before they could walk.[2] What they have done is even greater
than what was taught to them.'

The ideal student is God's gift—one who has given their employer
more than was taught to them. They act out truth because they chose
to live life appropriately, just as you come to me now in good health
and the King is content with all that has happened.

So take your years of living. What I have had on this earth is no
small matter: I have had a hundred and ten years of living allowed to
me, and the King's favours are now in the presence of my ancestors
because I acted out truth for the King right to the grave.[3]

So it ends, its start to its finish as was found in writing.[4]

1 Literally 'he has come from him in line with his body'.
2 Literally 'while he was still in the womb', which is a common enough
   phrase in this sense.
3 Literally 'the place of reverence'.
4 L1 had a little more which is now lost, including perhaps the copyist's name.

II. THE TEACHING OF KAGEMNI

A LL THAT REMAINS of *The Teaching of Kagemni* takes up the first two pages of P.Prisse (see pages 30–31). However, an unknown number of pages have been lost at the start and none of the missing text is known from another source, so the remainder is presented here essentially as a footnote to *The Teaching of Ptahhatp*.[1] Formally, none of the text has been written in red ink, so any division of the text into individual teachings has to be the interpretation of the translator guided by the grammatical structure.

There is genuine ambiguity within the text regarding the identity of the teacher. A summary epilogue reads as though it were added to the original Teaching, because it has a tone to the effect that this is how they did things in the old days ('they would put themselves on their bellies while exactly what was written was read aloud', etc.). Whether or not this is the case, the epilogue tells us that a vizier of King Huni, the last king of the Third Dynasty, is here teaching the next generation of the royal household. We also learn that later, after Huni had passed away and Snofru became king, Kagemni was confirmed as Vizier and Overseer of the City (see page 82). Does this suggest that Kagemni was one of the young students ('children' in the original)? If so, the teacher's name is lost to us: could he be Imhotep or Kairsu, both men named in the New Kingdom eulogy of writers whose teachings are otherwise unknown to us (see page 31)?[2] Sadly, the historical record does not furnish the name of any vizier of Huni. On the other hand, the vizier may be Kagemni himself, teaching the young Snofru, in which case his appointment following Snofru's accession would simply be confirming him in office—not least because of his proven wisdom. Would such a step be required? If the Teaching really does belong to the reign of Huni, then our Kagemni can hardly be the same Kagemni whose beautifully decorated tomb-chapel at Saqqara is familiar to tourists.[3] This man held the same high offices but under King Teti of the Sixth Dynasty, far too many decades later for the identification to hold. Conversely, if it were the same Kagemni, then the epilogue dating him to the time of Snofru, the greatest of all pyramid builders, is mistaken. Again, we simply do not know.

The text as we have it shares obvious themes with *The Teaching of Ptahhatp*, not least the self-defeating nature of greed and indulgence — which mentally and physically reduce a person; the need to hold your thoughts in company; the presence of God in anything that happens; and, of course, the need for a student to learn from a teacher. According to Sir Alan Gardiner, for example, 'the sage is preaching that a timid, retiring, taciturn nature finds the road open to free, unimpeded life'[4] and 'I find the call to suppression of self, to modesty, and to moderation permeating the book'.[5] There is also an instructional style recognizably similar to Ptahhatp's, such as introducing exemplary situations with the word 'whenever', which is perhaps sufficient to explain why the two books were compiled in a single volume. On the other hand, the obvious difference between them is the lack of summary conclusions in this instance, although the epilogue specifically states that the teacher is summarizing 'people and how their characters presented themselves to him'. Perhaps this teacher is simply stating what students need to learn, whereas Ptahhatp's teaching goes on to summarize all that he knows about people for a more mature audience, in the person of the king?

p. 1 **Teaching. On tact**

[An unknown number of teachings have been lost from the start]

A respectful person may well flourish but a scrupulous person will have gained the recognition.

The inner tent may open for whoever keeps quiet but the situation of the appreciative is the most comfortable.

Do not speak out: sharp are the knives facing anyone treading a particular path, and there is no progress to be made except at its proper moment.

Teaching. On greed

Whenever you sit down with lots of people, refuse the food you want. Saying no is only a moment but greed is objectionable—it gets pointed out.

A cup of water quenches the thirst, a mouthful of dried herbs fortifies. Something perfect stands for perfection, and a little something stands for a lot.

One whose appetite is voracious grows impotent as time goes by, and those in whose lives their appetite goes too far come to disdain them.

Teaching. On self-denial

Whenever you sit down with a glutton, you should eat once their greed has died down.

Whenever you drink with a drunkard, you should join in once their desire has been satisfied.

Do not get cross about the fine food the avaricious take for themselves—accept what they leave you, do not refuse it. Then there shall be harmony.

For someone free from an opinion about food, no words can affect them. Better to be one who keeps the eyes in check than one whose desire grows fat. Someone who is rude to their own mother would be nice to them—everybody cares for them.

Teaching. On humility

Let your reputation make its own way

p. 2 while you say nothing with your mouth, so that you may be asked for instead.

Do not be arrogant because you feel powerful among your peers in case you get attacked.

What may happen cannot be known, nor what God may do to fit how he disciplines.

Epilogue

So, the vizier would have these students of his summoned. After he had testified about the conduct of people and how their characters appeared to him, he would end by saying to them, 'All that is written in this book, listen to it as I say it. Do not misrepresent what has been set down.'

Then they would put themselves on their bellies while what was written was read aloud word for word; it would be better for their minds than anything else which is of this entire earth, and from then on they would stand and sit accordingly.

Eventually, the person of the hereditary and sovereign king Huni reached his mooring, when the person of the hereditary and sovereign king Snofru rose as the effective king by birth for this entire earth and Kagemni was put as Overseer of the City and Vizier.

So it ends.

III. THE TEACHING OF HORDEDEF

ALL THAT REMAINS of *The Teaching of Hordedef* are extracts written many centuries after the earliest copies of *The Teaching of Ptahhatp*—specifically, on sixteen ostraca dating from the late New Kingdom at Thebes. Some of these at least were written in Deyr al-Medinah, like various late copies of *The Teaching of Ptahhatp* (see page 52). There is also an extract on a small wooden board reportedly from a burial at Saqqara dating to the Late Period (see page 138), which means generally the period 664–323 BC.[6] Taking these extracts together, a putative text may be reconstructed but it preserves only the beginning of the Teaching.[7] At least as I read this text, each individual teaching (after the first) incorporates within it a saying or truism taken from elsewhere— presumably just something known more generally in contemporary society—though this is only stated as such on one occasion ('remember how they say' in the last teaching translated below). The same technique of using quotations is clearly also used, albeit less intentionally, in *The Teaching of Ptahhatp*.

Hordedef himself is named ahead of Ptahhatp in the New Kingdom eulogy of writers (see page 31) and today is conventionally identified as Hordjedef, a well-known son of the Fourth Dynasty king Khufu, who happens to be a character from the story written in Papyrus Westcar (see page 57).[8] That said, other than the similarity of the names there is little in the text to support this identification compellingly, so dating *The Teaching of Hordedef* earlier than *The Teaching of Ptahhatp* is only speculation. We can at least notice that the overarching theme of the Teaching as it survives (preparing a funerary endowment) is consistent with a principal theme in, for example, the Fourth Dynasty tomb inscriptions of Metjen and others discussed in Chapter 2. On the other hand, the old argument that the pithy formulation of the individual teachings in *Hordedef* is less 'evolved' than the instructional style of *Ptahhatp* and *Kagemni* is an opinion at best—a clear case of putting the evolutionary cart in front of its horse.[9] In fact, within pharaonic Egyptian literature the most obvious parallel to this laconic style would

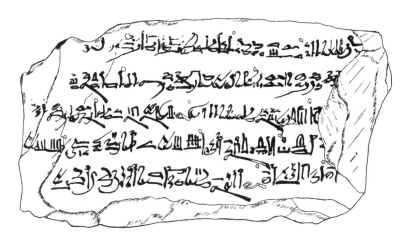

Copy of an ostracon, whose brief text actually comprises the first half of
The Teaching of Hordedef as we have it. Limestone. 25.5 cm (10 in.) wide.
Twentieth Dynasty. Thebes.

be *The Teaching of Onkhsheshonqy,* which is first known to us from a
Ptolemaic book.[10]

If only because the reconstructed text is so fragmentary and we have
no notion of how much has been lost after the beginning, it is difficult
to assess the relationship between this Teaching and those in P.Prisse.
Of course, Hordedef evokes the path of service and reward, including
that of 'being remembered for the rest of time', discussed in Chapter 2.
Being remembered features prominently in Ptahhatp's conclusions too,
though arguably there it is intended more broadly than the terms of
a funerary cult. As we have it here, Hordedef instructs his student to
prepare an 'estate' (a home and career): both for the sake of his wife,
who may then raise his children; and for his son, who may look after him
in due course. Beyond that, however, the student should provide himself
with a funerary endowment to furnish and supply a tomb-chapel ('make
your estate useful for the cemetery'). The final surviving remarks are
too disjointed to translate sensibly here but they give no indication that

Hordedef's teaching about the transformative value of preparing
for death, quoted on a wooden label from a burial. 14 cm (5½ in.) wide.
Late Period. Saqqara.

the Teaching ever moves on from this line of argument—for example,
we encounter the grim observation that 'one gets buried as a captive of
the cemetery'. Even a single fragmentary instruction that may seem to
point towards life in happy company ('choose a band of musicians for
yourself') is more than likely a reference to funerary ceremonies.

In a sense, this is a simple reminder to look clearly to the future and
prepare for what is bound to come ('let what is in sight of your eyes
keep you pure'). However, the most striking aspect of this teaching
picks up another crucial word from *The Teaching of Ptahhatp*: how you
prepare for your death is more important for your future than how your
parents first provided for your life, because a funerary endowment
'transforms you more than inheritance does' (plate XII). Much more
obviously than Ptahhatp, therefore, Hordedef is using the Egyptian
verb 'transform' ('*akh*) to indicate a change of state after death—a
transformation he then immediately links with the Egyptian funerary cult of food-offerings. Remarkably, a much later song from a New
Kingdom tomb brings a pointed rejoinder: 'I have heard the sayings
of Imhotep and Hordedef, whose words people still speak so often.
Where are their places? Their walls have fallen down, the remains of
them lost as though they had never been.'

Beginning of the teaching made by the elite-member, community-leader and king's son Hordedef for his son named Awibra, as he says:

Let what is in sight of your eyes keep you pure because another person cannot keep you pure.

If you would do well, prepare your own estate, which makes your wife for you a lady of substance that a male child may be born to you. You should build your estate solid for your son — 'You have made the place where you may live.'

Make your estate useful for the cemetery. Make your situation in the west excellent. Death to us means getting fodder, and getting ourselves fertile ground requires the living — 'The estate of the dead belongs to the living.'

Find yourself an allotment, a bit of land irrigated <more efficiently> than marshes, for ploughing rather than fishing and fowling — 'Once the time of passing away has happened, one eats as one makes with one's own hands.' You should provide your own wreaths, the relevant funerary director and a spirit-priest for the tomb-chapel, so they can pour spring water for you as someone with an exceptional legacy.

Choose the allotment from the best of your lands, watered all year round. This transforms you more than inheritance does, so make it better than ... ... Remember how they say, 'Being remembered for the rest of time is not inherited.'

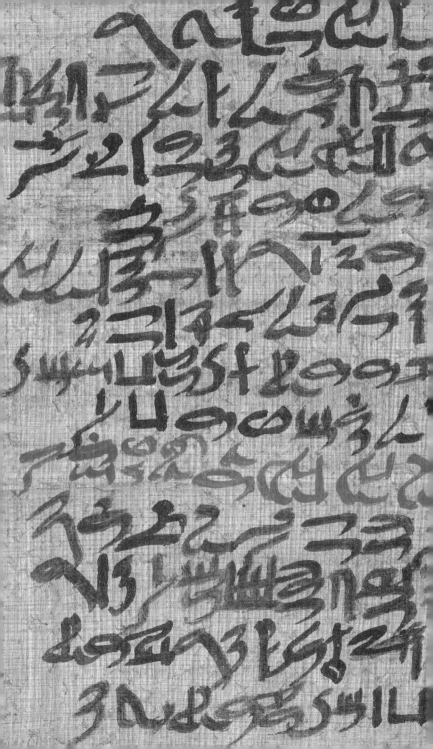

4

THE TEACHER,
PTAHHATP

*When a learned man is presented with any statement
in an ancient author, the one question he never asks
is whether it is true.*

C. S. LEWIS,
The Screwtape Letters (1942), Letter 27

I S I T E V E N credible that the modern world has lessons to learn from the ancient world? Surely we left our ancestors behind long ago, evolved and went on to become a wiser, happier and more mature species as a consequence? Did we not? In his 1906 edition of *The Oldest Books in the World* Battiscombe Gunn noted the irony that,

> great age hallows all things, even the most mean, investing them with a certain sanctity; and the little sandal of a nameless child, or the rude amulet placed long ago with weeping on the still bosom of a friend, will move his heart as strongly by its appeal as the proud and enduring monument of a great conqueror.[1]

On the other hand, this never seems to be true of what the ancients *wrote*:

> so few are the voices across so great a span of years that those among them having anything to tell us should be welcome exceedingly; whereas, for the most part, they have cried in the wilderness of neglect hitherto, or fallen on ears filled with the clamour of more instant things.[2]

Evidently it is one thing to travel on holiday and stare admiringly at a ruinous pyramid, but to read an intact ancient book from first page to last requires a different kind of commitment — and presumably different expectations of what we may gain from the experience. So, the one thing we do not do is listen to the words, and the reasons why are threefold at least.

Old age and obscurity

First, as we have already mentioned, 'the oldest book in the world' came to light just when scholars were beginning to explain human history in terms of evolution. Indeed, it was a moment when some committed scholars were actually finding themselves disappointed by how little the newly deciphered ancient Egyptian scripts apparently had to tell us.[3] For example, having played a key role in the decipherment story himself, the brilliant scientist and physician Thomas Young (1773–1829) wrote to a friend that 'the inscriptions on temples, and the generality of manuscripts found with the mummies, appear to relate to their ridiculous rites and ceremonies'.[4] In a sense he is entirely correct: the texts that survive from pharaonic Egypt are mostly funerary inscriptions or temple inscriptions, which talk about the relationship between the king and the gods—and even then not in theological terms but in terms of their rites and ceremonies, however ridiculous. In reality, though, this unwillingness to ignore whatever the ancient past had to say was more than simply an aspect of scholarship: more than seventy years ago the great Belfast-born essayist C. S. Lewis (1898–1963) noted that we have to distinguish popular 'evolutionism', such as we are liable to encounter on the television, from the rigorous scientific arguments ascribed to Darwin or anyone else because 'if science had not met the imaginative need, science would not have been so popular'.[5] In other words, we wanted to be told that there are good scientific reasons to leave our ancestors behind, which is an issue we will return to in the next chapter.

Now, if the times did not need to acknowledge 'the oldest book in the world', then the obscurity of the manuscripts was a second compelling reason to crown its irrelevance. The text of *The Teaching of Ptahhatp* itself is a notorious challenge, described by Gustave Jéquier, its first modern editor, as 'the most difficult Egyptian literary text to translate',[6] while even Sir Alan Gardiner looked for no more than a 'glimmer of daylight'.[7] In 1931, the Egyptologist Eric Peet (1882–1934) ascribed this state of affairs to our uncertain understanding of Ancient Egyptian words.[8] In a sense, Peet's comment only highlights the unexpected nature of *The Teaching*, which turns out to be about anything but the usual 'rites and ceremonies'. Still, there is more to the difficulty than this: for example, some of Ptahhatp's sayings rely on word-plays, which were an integral aspect of the meaning of words for the ancients but are almost bound to be lost in translation.

One especially sceptical tradition has been draped like a pall over the two centuries of Egyptology. According to this 'philological' tradition, an ancient book such as *The Teaching of Ptahhatp* is an archaeological artefact—a mere sliver of an alien culture, no more meaningful than a broken pot or a child's sandal because we can never know the intentions of its author nor grasp the cultural implications of its words in their fullness. Up to a point, this would also be true of the Old Testament, but (according to this tradition) there is a cultural schism separating us from ancient Egypt that, unlike the case of the Old Testament, has not been bridged by continuous use and translation. As a consequence, *The Teaching* has been cut off from us by history and geography and by creeping human progress. Now this is quite true, of course, unless Ptahhatp is somehow speaking to matters that are not confined by time and space, and if not everything a human being can learn is a mindless biological instinct or a cultural construct. Perhaps a wise, ancient book has the capacity to speak to a timeless human spirit precisely because it has crossed millennia. Gardiner, for one, noted 'that our translations, though very liable to error in detail, nevertheless at the worst give a roughly adequate idea of what the ancient author intended'.[9] In other words, we can translate an ancient book from a foreign language just as sensibly as we can translate a modern one—or, to put this another way, *The Teaching of Ptahhatp* has been translated several times since 1931, so there has to be a sense in which some experts believe translation can be achieved. The real issue becomes whether it is worthwhile to do so.

This is not just a question of antiquity either, because older Egyptian texts have been read, often by students starting out in Egyptology and, therefore, with relatively little experience of ancient texts. Nor is it a question of genre—*The Teaching of Kagemni*, by comparison, seems straightforward to read in the original Ancient Egyptian. On the other hand, the Egyptian text of *The Teaching of Ptahhatp* is a dense, challenging read ripe with uncommon words and perplexing ideas, and in our own culture we are liable to ascribe an especially difficult book to the category of badly written or very clever. I could rewrite the present book using words like mimesis, ontology and epistemology and you would quickly consign it to one or the other category—or both! Of course, when a book is most ancient the possibility that it is very clever in our terms may be excluded, so...

To complicate matters, *The Teaching of Ptahhatp* is undoubtedly founded in the spiritual nature of the human condition—as the Dutch

Egyptologist and Christian minister Adriaan de Buck (1892–1959) had already noted in 1932[10]—whereas questions of metaphysics and spirituality did not always sit well with nineteenth- and twentieth-century sceptical traditions. To this day, the problem of meaning raised by Ptahhatp (that is, the simple fact that things have meaning) has never been formally addressed within the discipline of Egyptology, while the nature of the human soul or spirit and its relationship with truth —effectively treated as a truism in ancient texts—has all but fallen off the 'Philosophy' shelves in modern libraries and bookshops. Almost by definition, a mention of the soul or spirit characterizes a book as irremediably old-fashioned or else 'New Age'.

To add to this uneasy picture, there is undoubtedly a prejudice liable to lead any of us on slender grounds to laud or condemn books we have never actually read, presumably in order to justify our unwillingness or inability to find the time to do so while still maintaining an air of general learning. James Clerk Maxwell (1831–1879), Edinburgh-born scientist and father of electromagnetism, noted the tendency in discussing books that 'sceptics pretend to have read them, and have found certain witty objections ... which too many of the orthodox unread admit, and shut up the subject as haunted'.[11] Often it is the prospect of the Bible or the Quran that we object to, not our familiarity with it. Likewise, our received opinions of Shakespeare, Darwin, Marx or Hawking are what we promote, not our well-rounded appreciation of their written works. As we have seen, Socrates condemns this attitude—but so does Ptahhatp, even more emphatically: 'Repeat only statements of fact,' he says, 'rather than listening to a world of piss-taking.' Learn for yourself, he says, so 'if you want to find out about your colleague's character, do not ask around, go to them. Take a moment with them alone until you are no longer unsure on the matter.' Is there no sense in which this advice could apply to the business of getting to know your own ancestors?

To take an important example, if *The Teaching of Ptahhatp* has gained any traction in modern culture it has done so because the Thirty-Second Teaching is conventionally presented as a condemnation of homosexuality. As such the book seems all too obviously out of step with our own attitudes, albeit in different ways at different times. Gunn's 1906 edition deleted the teaching altogether in favour of the note '[Concerning unnatural sin]', and he was not the last to leave it out. Surprisingly, this interpretation has persisted despite our increasing awareness that there is no other reference (good, bad or indifferent) to homosexuality in ancient Egyptian texts, apart from a single, surreal mythological reference to a sexual assault.[12] To be clear, this is not to suggest that homosexuality was unheard of in pharaonic Egypt, only that it is not mentioned—there are no mentions of spiders in texts either but what conclusion do we draw from that fact? In truth, Ptahhatp's reference is to sex with a juvenile—literally a 'woman child' (*ḥemt kherd*) from which has been derived the improbable reading 'ladyboy'.[13] The latter reading seems even more unnecessary in view of Ptahhatp's subsequent comment that again refers to the immature or impressionable ('With the immature you know what is condemned'). In other words, there is no need whatsoever to conflate homosexuality and paedophilia in order to explain the thrust of Ptahhatp's condemnation, which he supports with two observations again referring more obviously to paedophilia. First, that desires entailing sexual gratification through the abuse of children are obviously wrong and known to be wrong by the perpetrator—no more need be said. Secondly, that paedophilia is self-defeating because its practice will not bring relief from the attendant desires. The point of this example? That the principal received impression of *The Teaching of Ptahhatp* in modern culture is a wholly misleading impression but conveniently has been one to 'shut up the subject as haunted'.

If this bleak observation on the dark side of human conduct is easy to translate across time and space, some of Ptahhatp's lessons seem wholly problematic for us not so much to understand but to accept. For example, his very last teaching sets out the premise of marrying 'a cheat, shameless and known to the town—duplicitous, prefers the time spent apart'. Of course, this resonates deep within our own culture and immediately raises the spectres of separation and divorce. 'Do not throw them out' teaches Ptahhatp, unexpectedly. One distinguished commentator sees in this comment an invitation to seek solace in 'unconventional' lifestyles, suggesting that ancient lifestyles were 'unexpectedly varied' in any case.[14] Swinging, even! In truth, this is the kind of scholarly rationalization that reflects well on nobody. After all, in Ptahhatp's ultimate scenario the facts are spare and bleak: your spouse is shameless and faithless, and your neighbours are laughing at you. What greater humiliation could there be? What betrayal more profound? Who can easily bear to hear Shakespeare retelling the tortured thoughts of the cuckold: 'Perchance he spoke not, but, like a full-acorn'd boar, a German one, cried "O!" and mounted'?[15] Do we honestly believe such bitter resentments cut less deeply in ancient peoples? Is there really solace here to be found in teaching 'if you can't beat 'em'?

Surely not. However, *The Teaching of Ptahhatp* does not finally tell you what to do with the cheat—it simply asks you to do whatever you do without rancour or abuse. Reeling from the bitterest blow to the ego, Ptahhatp advises you to consider your own state of mind because 'shamelessness tests your equanimity'. Otherwise the outcome, all too predictably, is not going to be divorce but resentment, violence, even murder—Hollywood has made an industry out of retelling this tale. The extremity of the provocation is the crux of this ultimate teaching: utter confusion, unchained emotions and, most of all, the belief that I do not deserve this—that I should not have to endure outcomes that sadly happen to other people all the time. If we step back from the practical business of divorce, we hear emotional echoes deep in the experience of our own relationships with others and with ourselves—echoes perhaps in a comment by the Irish writer Brian Keenan that 'if we are in touch with the soul-side of our personality we may not commit evil, and if we did I am sure the psychic pain would be worse than any prison'.[16]

Undoubtedly, the teachings of many great teachers may be easier to read than put into practice or there would be no call for teaching from experience. As Ptahhatp says, his kind of teaching is an empirical measure of what people ought to do for their own benefit because,

> If you listen to the things I have said to you, so all your prospects improve. Their demonstration of truth is their value.

There is an education here in his teaching, which is 'transformative for whoever will listen, hobbling whoever tries to step over it'. First and foremost, according to Ptahhatp, knowledge is grounded in truth and 'truth is ever important, ever relevant. It has not been changed since the beginning of time'. In other words, truth stands apart from the caprices of human history or human wilfulness. When human conduct is detached from truth, the conduct itself becomes a means for the destruction of a person's harmony, a cause of prevarication for even the strongest or calmest, and a source of suffering and unhappiness. As we shall discuss in Chapter 5, in an ancient account of reality the principles of the world (the laws of physics, mathematics, justice and so on) are what is fixed and it is the people and things we see around us that are shifting and impermanent. The world of the mind and body is literally momentary, our desires are fleeting, whereas the spirit perceives the timeless principles of truth. Accordingly, a human community is bound to be governed by principles woven through the fabric of creation—principles that can be learned and understood—so wise behaviour 'is set at the standard, all its conduct measured from plumb' and may lead us, like Ptahhatp, to Izezi's palace where we should 'stand and sit at the appropriate moments. The very first day has been arranged for you.' In the presence of the king—which, in our terms, is more akin to a law court or church than a government office—we see not what is now but what has always been and this is the measure of truth, whereas 'crookedness has never established itself as the standard'. We judge wrong from right, not the other way round.

Still, principles can only be overstepped because each of us is free to do so. Anybody may or may not recognize facts—may or may not behave wisely—but matters of fact cannot be manipulated as a result. The difficulty of setting oneself against this reality is the inevitable outcome—'What will be will be. There is no escaping what is in store for us' because 'anyone who oversteps principles meets with consequences, which is what the greedy overlook'. Inevitable in the sense that the outcome is always the same in practice—confusion or frustration or sickness or conflict for people who 'instead of what would raise them they do everything demeaning. They live on what kills us, and what they consume is morbid.' A person is free to walk off the top of a house but the fact of gravity may cause them to regret their choice. Too much of a good thing will do the same. A person whose conduct is wrong may refuse to accept that fact but, according to Ptahhatp, they are still wrong and will suffer spiritually as a consequence: 'Great are the thoughts given by God but whoever listens to their appetite belongs to an enemy.'

God and facts

Which brings us to the third good reason not to listen to *The Teaching of Ptahhatp* any more—the presence of God in the book. Now, the book is not religious insofar as it is not concerned with the worship of a god or gods, nor with the nature of divinity. Instead, Ptahhatp simply assumes the fact of an intentional creator, which is divine and therefore external to the human mind, as the basis for explaining the facts of reality, and especially the fact that the world makes sense. The 'fact' of God simply serves as the basis for Ptahhatp's conclusions and allows him to establish for the first time in history the principle of timeless, unchanging truth as the basis for the meaning of things—a belief explained more formally in the ancient account of the relationship between words and meaning in Chapter 5.

For instance, we can take the example of Ptahhatp's comments about fear and coercion. Even for a person in authority, fear achieves nothing because 'what people fear has never yet happened—only what God requires happens' and 'God responds accordingly'. In other words, neither causing fear nor being afraid actually brings anything about, so supposing that you are powerful and seeking to rule by fear is a profound self-deception: 'When someone says "I am powerful", they are saying "I am trapped in my self-importance"'. Whatever happens happens in terms of the God-given principles, so those who seek to control others by fear, in doing so reveal how diminished they are because 'they end up given over to what they cannot control'. Therefore, 'do not give an order that is not appropriate. Confrontation brings in conflict.' The ulti-mate deceit of force is to suggest it is not futile, even in the matter of instructing others: 'Discipline from the head, educate from the character ... Any (use of force) other than against an offence only causes someone in the wrong to resent you.' Likewise, do not seek power that has not come to you because 'the employer of a whole workforce may pray to only have to follow.' In any event, for anyone in a position of responsibility 'it does not hurt to roll up your sleeves'.

Throughout the teachings we gather that this deceit is not just true of fear and coercion but of any worldly advantage because, after all, 'do you not stand in a line behind someone else just like you, for whom the same things have already happened?' Least of all are you able to force someone to love you: so, in a relationship with a wife 'keep away from her the kind of control that constrains her' because 'this is about keeping her in your home, about you retaining her devotion'; and in the case of friends and colleagues 'for the love of you to endure it must do so in the bellies of those who really do love you'. Accordingly, Ptahhatp says, 'when you hold power create respect by knowing your business and by speaking calmly' and 'resolve to live happily and whatever is given will come of its own accord'.

The word here translated 'God' (*netjer*) is written throughout *The Teaching* without an article ('a' or 'the'), which is standard for nouns in the language of the Old and Middle Kingdoms — just as it is typical, for example, in Latin or Russian. Therefore, the word may be translated into English as 'a god' or 'the god'. However, Ptahhatp makes no reference to gods (plural) anywhere, while the two times he names gods (Osiris and Horus) are simply uses of set phrases. Otherwise, the absence of gods' names or gods in the plural is noteworthy. For instance, the reign of King Akhenaten (*c*. 1353–1336 BC), centuries later in pharaonic history, has somehow become identified with a popular narrative about the king's supposed conversion to monotheism — that is, a belief in one sole god. The narrative of Akhenaten as a visionary monotheist has long since passed into popular culture through the works of intellectuals and artists such as Thomas Mann, Sigmund Freud, Philip Glass and Naguib Mahfouz. In reality, texts from Akhenaten's reign use the names of many different gods, whereas, centuries earlier, Ptahhatp relies on the presence of a single creator as the basis for explaining the meaning of things. The point is this: ancient Egyptian gods are not simple, well-defined creatures—certainly not in the manner that you, the ground beneath your house, or the book you are reading are simple creatures. Ancient Egyptian gods are (were?) real, potent and affect us, just as words and winds do. However, like words and winds, they are not independent of a context: if the context happens to be an image in a temple of the king embracing a god, then—as with the wings of an angel in medieval art—the artist gives the Egyptian god a human body. Nonetheless, its body is a function of the art, not a feature of the actual god. In Western terms, I suppose an Egyptian god has the form and face of the wind or a photon—which is what, exactly? More to the point, the gods (plural) are still creatures too—that is, they too have a creator, which is Ptahhatp's God, as we will discuss further in the next chapter.

Now, in temples and funerary inscriptions the relationship between divinity and humanity is expressed principally through kingship, as the earliest and foremost office of humanity (see pages 91 and 110), and it is defined in reciprocal terms as 'love' and 'praise'. In *The Teaching of Ptahhatp*, however, the same relationship is expressed through spiritual growth leading to good conduct; through the humility required of each of us to act out the God-given truth; and through the possibility of learning from every event by evaluating the facts until we finally become wise through service. Wisdom is not simply a function of education, as noted in Ptahhatp's most quoted remark, 'wise words are rarer than malachite yet found among the girls at the grindstones'. The humble individual is wise because they recognize and put faith in their God-given gifts and treat others accordingly with respect: 'If you cultivate flowers in the marshes, God has done great things through you. Do not talk yourself up with those close to you' because 'gladness does not come with home delivery: when it is not there, trusted friends have to come over'.

On the other hand, if it is natural that each of us is free to act out or to overstep truth, it is vain and futile for us to seek to convince even those of our own children 'who are stranded' and 'do not seek a ferry'. Cyberspace is pulsing with the opinions of men and women who claim not to need others to tell them how to think, but for anyone to engage with others, to be open to others, they must find common ground to stand on. For this common ground, Ptahhatp makes his appeal to the simple truth, which is out of time and transcendent and therefore not a matter of opinion, as the secure foundation on which human beings reach out to one another. It is just not for us to determine another person's relationship with the truth.

Of course, you are liable to meet 'someone looking for an argument' every day—online, on the television, at work, at home. As the modern aphorism goes, life is short so it is important to spend as much of it as possible arguing with strangers in cyberspace. In truth, your wisest course of action is to walk away because argument does not establish facts—only the uneven relationship of those arguing. A clever person will defeat your arguments, irrespective of who is actually correct, so 'make little of nonsense by not getting into an argument with them'. Then again, a person who can match your arguments allows you no possibility of achieving anything with words so 'show that you are better than them with silence'. This leaves only the person you can master in an argument but, in turn, such a situation only allows you to indulge your ego because 'humiliating the hapless is perverse, and you are going to get what you want anyway'. In any scenario, argument does not affect the truth, only your relationship with the truth—and your own relationship with the truth should be all that matters to you. In confrontation, the only thinking and behaviour you can affect is your own and 'just as you disagree with them, they are not going to agree with you'. You are not required to give in to whoever wants an argument but simply 'reach out your hand and bow politely' before withdrawing to 'let your self-restraint match their advantages'.

Alternatively, if someone approaches you on a particular matter, then hear what they have to say because 'not everything people ask you for can happen but the purpose of listening is to clear the air'. After all, 'those who rely on you need to say what is on their mind even more than they need to get something done about it'. Although you can only influence or affect the person facing you by your example because 'every person, who is a teacher by the way they act, passes on as much to the next generation', nonetheless 'show character, do not pass on your flaws. Let truth be apparent so that the next generation may thrive.' In the end, facts amount to the true nature of the world and contemplation of meaning is the only way to learn the facts. Therefore, 'whenever you are in charge, accountable for the circumstances of many, seek the meaning for you in every event until your conduct becomes impeccable.' Eventually, 'if an instance of the ideal happens through one who is in charge, they are meaningful for eternity. All their wisdom is for all of time.' Of course, we know that empty wagons clatter and groan most, and the people who know least often have the loudest voices and the longest explanations, so Ptahhatp specifically warns that 'your silence is more effective than guessing. You should say only what you know how to explain.' This is more than advice about how to avoid embarrassing yourself at work—it is a humble attitude to life because,

> Listening is what God wants, and one who does not listen hates God. Listening or not listening is a choice and a person's choice is life, prosperity and health to them. A listener surely listens and speaks as such, but a lover of listening is one who acts on what was said.

In other words, the authentic purpose of human language is not to talk but to listen—listen and learn to behave accordingly.

Power and pretence

Having discussed the futility of argument, Ptahhatp becomes the first of many teachers in history to spell out the reciprocal connection between power and responsibility. However, he immediately defines responsible conduct as the commitment to self-awareness and self-improvement. Improvement comes through education, in the literal sense of drawing out the meaning of everything that happens, so a teacher with a student 'should let their own innate wisdom come out of them, and in the presence of their spirit there is benefit for you too'. For obvious reasons, 'the restraint of force is going to bring out the real character'—the truth of a person cannot be beaten into them because, as the great Danish philosopher Søren Kierkegaard (1813–1855) put it, 'every person is primitively planned to be a self, appointed to become oneself'.[17] Since truth is unchanging, the ultimate outcome of self-improvement is to attain the conduct that serves as an example to everyone—which is exactly what Ptahhatp summarizes in his seven conclusions.

This is a straightforward position but far from simple in its implications. The impulse to find meaning is not a licence to impose your own meaning on whatever happens. Instead, Ptahhatp emphasizes, we must practise how to pay attention to the meaning of events by trusting our mental faculties rather than by talking or by listening to the opinions of others: 'Trust your mind all the time of your being. Do not add to what has already been said' because 'genuine understanding is there before your eyes'. This is especially true in company where, for instance, 'clarity can never come about amid praise'—by which we surely understand sycophancy. Only by paying close attention do we discover facts, and facts reveal fundamental truths about the human condition, even though, as we noted, 'listening or not listening is a choice'. Since truth has never changed and wrong is never right, and since we can establish (from Ptahhatp himself!) that this has been the case since the beginning of history, no one can look beyond themselves to explain why troubles fall on them. Human lives are, and always have been, products of our own choices but we still feel the need to lay blame and make excuses: 'whoever says "I have got myself caught" never admits that "I got caught because of my own choices"'. Around AD 400 an Egyptian monk made the same point this way: 'In any adversity do not blame others—find fault only with yourself, saying, "This is happening to me because of my mistakes."'[18] We cannot control life but we can control our responses to it, and we can learn from others and from what has happened, so 'smile all the time of your being. Whatever has left the store cannot go back in'. In humility the individual chooses not to be who we would wish to be but to become through experience the individual of God-given gifts, so 'the educated person is the one who nurtures their soul by realizing on earth the ideal self within'.

Wisely or not, we make our choices and can only ever be secure in what we have earned, so Ptahhatp reserves particular scorn for gossip, greed and pretence. 'You should not repeat gossip' he says '... this is ruination from fantasy', but instead 'repeat only statements of fact'. Gossip comes from jealousy and is a danger to the gossiper as much as to the victim because 'when a theft gets ordered to be done, the one who does the thieving is the one sentenced in law'. Other self-destructive desires such as jealousy can never be gratified, not in the long term and least of all sexually when 'the mere moment seems to be a dream but you can go to your grave still thinking about it'. Meanwhile, he could hardly be more plain in teaching that greed 'is a sick infestation for which there is no cure' and its corruption will set even family members against one another. Simply surrender your claims on the material world and 'do not covet even your own slice' because 'only bread meant for sharing provokes resentment'. If what is yours by right is there for you, then good. If not, then your loss should not distort your sense of what is right—for this to happen would be both the definition of greed and the price of greed. If greed betrays what is lacking in the character of the greedy, no amount of success can ever make this right because 'there is a thought that listens to its appetite and puts its wants where its needs should be, and so its mind gets wasted and its body reduced' until 'the greedy leave no leftovers behind'—comments that are obviously also quips about excessive consumption. Such excess also includes intellectual theft and pretending to be more accomplished than we really are, because greed is not simply wanting more for ourselves but about wanting to be regarded as more than we are, whereas 'whoever makes themself out to be more important than their actual achievements is the one who gets embarrassed. If anyone would rather show discipline, they stop speaking at "I have said my piece."' Conveniently, all this talk of greed and pretence brings us to the dinner table—to good food and good company—and, arguably, to the biggest challenge Ptahhatp has for us today with regard to the human condition and the meaning of life.

Company and the spirit

The most striking aspect of *The Teaching of Ptahhatp* for the modern world is the ancient Egyptian concept of the presence or 'spirit' (*ka*), which is discussed at least a dozen times in the book. The very idea may seem to lead us towards the tomb, quite literally because the pharaonic offering cult, discussed in Chapter 2, is likewise directed towards the spirit of the deceased. In the tomb, your spirit is typically defined by your name, your image, your job titles and your family relationships. In other words, the spirit is that aspect of yourself present to others—the outward-facing you. When people made funerary offerings in your tomb, they did so for your *ka*. Now, as we have noted already, the great majority of the written material that has come down to us from ancient Egypt has come from temples or tombs. We can go further and emphasize that what we have is even more limited because most temple inscriptions are to do with ceremonies and most tomb inscriptions are to do with offerings, which is precisely what Thomas Young complained about 200 years ago. Likewise, all the earliest instances of ancient Egyptian literature come from a funerary context, typically at Luxor. So can we actually separate literary books from the tomb and from tomb inscriptions?[19] To suggest that ancient literature is somehow independent of any specific context and meant to be read for its sheer enjoyment presupposes that we understand what the books we have were intended for, by whoever copied them and by whoever took them to the grave—and we do not honestly know what that was. Copies of *The Teaching of Ptahhatp* on ostraca from Deyr al-Medinah during the New Kingdom only add to the intrigue because Deyr al-Medinah was a living community but a community, crucially, of funerary artists (see page 34).[20]

Obviously, this raises the question of what relevance a book such as *The Teaching of Ptahhatp* may have for the tomb. Is the answer simply the anthropologist's standard comment that someone wished to be buried with evidence of their literacy? Certainly literary books were interred beside—or even copied out in the same scroll as—other kinds of documents, including letters, business accounts, calendars, lists of

medical treatments and word-lists. Then again, other than an archaeologist, who was ever going to see these things? So is *The Teaching of
Ptahhatp* itself essentially about death rather than life? Undoubtedly, a
notable aspect of the book is the concept of transformation (*'akh*): the
teachings are intended to be 'transformative for whoever will listen'
because 'truth is transformative', and a teacher 'whose lips are precise
when speaking and their eyes in seeing, their ears accurate in hearing
what is transformative for their student—is one who acts out truth free
from error'. Simply put, 'listening transforms the listener', whereas
imposing your will on colleagues 'is not how to transform them'. The
point being that in *The Teaching of Hordedef* this same transformation
(*'akh*) is specifically connected to death insofar as a funerary endowment 'transforms you more than inheritance does'.

However, we can approach this connection to the spirit from another
angle, by turning to one of Ptahhatp's teachings which, at first glance
at least, seems to be entirely about this world and about life this side of
death—his Seventh Teaching, which is about dining in the company
of 'someone more important than you'. This is typically explained as a
warning about being shamelessly ambitious while building a career, and
it most certainly does identify ambition with greed. Still, here we are
now in the modern world and how can we possibly take seriously what
Ptahhatp has to say about God present at the table—not to mention
his chatter about spirits reaching out their arms? There may be some
insight into what he means to be found in context: the teachings immediately preceding this one include his initial teachings about the futility
of argument and the virtue of polite silence, following which we are
introduced to the crucial topics of responsibility, greed and the greedy
person. In *The Teaching of Kagemni* too we are told that when we dine in
company we all recognize those among us who are not greedy, noting
that 'someone who is rude to his own mother would be nice to them'. The
reverse of this, as we know, is that there is a price to pay for conduct that
seeks to obtain more than is intended for you, so 'grabbing' (whether
at influence or at food) is a 'spiritual offence'. Subsequently, in the
Eighth Teaching, the act of putting words into someone else's mouth or

misrepresenting the truth to others is likewise a spiritual offence. 'Stick to the facts,' Ptahhatp says, 'without introducing a point of view from someone else's opinions—important or trivial, it is a spiritual offence'. It would be tempting to translate 'spiritual offence' in each instance using the modern term 'sin', but in neither teaching is there necessarily any transgression of a law or a moral code—rather they seem to be simply examples of conduct that is self-defeating. In the Eleventh Teaching we are told that not trusting your spirit 'at all times' is also a spiritual offence. We see this self-defeating conduct at the dining table, just as we do in an argument, in an abusive relationship and so on.

Nevertheless, the intriguing aspect of the Seventh Teaching is not so much to learn about spiritual offence but to learn that spirits give just as God gives. At a social event, no one is so entitled that they 'just get' but 'when the night's business happens, it is the spirit that reaches out its arms'. The point being that at the table, even in the most cryptic allegory, we are not discussing the spirit in death—the spirit as we meet it in an Egyptian tomb—but the spirit in life, and specifically the possibility of spiritual gain when we are in good company—'as there is contentment in the presence of their spirits, there is only opposition in the presence of enemies'. When spirits reach out, how much comes to us, we are told, is 'based on God's plan'; and, if you benefit, then 'know your plumage when wealth is yours. Do not be miserly to your friends' because friends 'are greater than one's riches, and the wealth of each other'. At the end of the day, with the most important people as much as with friends 'a bellyful of love is more than satisfying—it puts clothes on your back'. In other words, dining (or any other moment in company) is a moment for either the spiritual growth or the spiritual offence that arises precisely because the moment is shared. We gain spiritually because the spirits of others give to us—we can grab at materials but we cannot grab love. On the other hand, apart from God's gift of creation there is no moment together because there is no timeless truth that provides the common ground on which we meet as spirits. We should note too that the funerary offering cult relied on the fact that those who love us maintain these spiritual relationships beyond death, which is the point raised by Hordedef.

Now, here there are aspects of Ptahhatp's account of the human social condition that we easily recognize. Love we know about, and friendship too. He also describes the impact of past experiences on our present behaviour in company: 'If their past experience comes out of them—they do things that make you indisposed to them or even to being friendly at all—do not be haughty, be measured.' This is something we would explain today in psychoanalytic terms. Likewise, when *The Teaching of Kagemni* notes that 'the inner tent may open for whoever keeps quiet but the situation of the appreciative is the most comfortable', we can hear in this the growing confidence that one person may have in letting another get close to them—and not only in a literal sense. However, the relationship between the human mind and others can be described very differently in ancient Egyptian terms. To take a stark example, a New Kingdom letter from a man to his wife, written three years after she died, strikes a dramatically unfamiliar tone for modern ears:

> What wrong have I done to you that I have been brought to this sad state I am in? What have I done to you? What you have done is grab hold of me, though I have done no harm to you. For, since I lived with you as your husband until today, what have I done to you that I must hide?[21]

If such anxiety affected a modern patient, presumably we would describe it as an attack of grief, conscience or something more sinister, from within the mind. However, this is our particular analysis. In his own account of his situation, this ancient Egyptian recognizes an external source for his mental disturbance—his dead wife, whose spirit, entirely contrary to Ptahhatp's Twenty-first Teaching, is exercising 'the kind of control that constrains him'. His letter illustrates how ancient Egyptian accounts of the human mind are both like our own and different, partly again for reasons we will discuss in the next chapter. For the moment, we can perhaps admit that their accounts are not necessarily less credible than ours because, faced with the question 'what is the mind?', we are still liable to have to reply that 'there is a lot of philosophical and scientific work to do before we can see where the answer lies'.[22]

In our present culture of radical self-possession, in which we assert the right to be self-created individuals, it is almost provocative to see the human condition described in a way that so much of who we really are is a spirit interacting with others in the moment; and though 'a spirit may relax with whoever loves it—it is about spirits giving along with God'. Yet, albeit in very specific senses, we still accept today that we are partly made up of others: for example, we are all the gift of our parents, so we recognize what Ptahhatp means when he talks about 'your child, who your spirit pours out for you' and when he notes that a characteristic such as 'true integrity gets passed on'. We may even accept that a part of who we are has come about from the inspiration of others, a matter which we will return to in the next chapter. Ptahhatp puts great stock in the human capacity to inspire and develop others, so 'choose your comments and inspire every mind to excellence' because 'a hothead's steam drifts all over but composure lays out its path'. On the other hand, 'Whoever worries all day will not inspire one positive moment. Whoever hides away all day will not build leadership.' We perhaps also recognize the shared experience when we are moved almost to tears by something profound in conversation or in music or in literature, knowing just as surely that we are moved by a momentary awareness of the timeless truth we share in common—a glimpse of what 'really means something'.

As such, ordinary life speaks to the fact that human beings are naturally part of a meaningful world and naturally belong with others. *The Teaching of Ptahhatp* maintains that the world can only have meaning because it is founded on timeless truth, so 'whoever listens and learns makes sense from deep within and is long remembered'. Language is for listening, and teaching should be by example—unless, like Ptahhatp here, you are required by some authority to state your case. He intends for us to learn the reality of life, not what happens when we die—though the handful of surviving copies have come to us from out of the tomb because his book promises a path of transformation and spiritual growth, whereby death need not be the end of our relationships nor our contributions to life. His approach is empirical, relies on our mental faculties and demands no proofs other than efficacy—what consistently works, which, if nothing else about his book, should give us pause for thought. By paying close attention to events, he asserts, we discover facts, and facts reveal the truth about our human condition—'there are no real riches without knowing them'. Wisely or not, we each of us make our choices, reap what we sow and can only be comfortable with what we have honestly earned, so 'do not misrepresent your success, which has happened for you out of God's gifts'. Likewise, whatever others may do, we can choose to smile, to avoid confrontation and to rejoice in our own fairness, fidelity and conscientious effort. After all, the alternatives are only choices too—but grimmer choices. In any case, we are always 'of the moment' and each and every moment is shared with others—so, however much material wealth we consume, it is of no benefit to us until we learn how to conduct ourselves in the company of others. Good conduct is what brings true benefit because our meaningful, spiritual relationships do not come and go with the moment, and without other people we cannot grow spiritually. So 'take your time' and 'take your years of living' and understand that life is not the business of the belly or even the mouth—'what wants to listen is the spirit'. So the question then becomes, what is it listening for?

5

WHY THINGS HAPPEN

*Surely nothing has come from
itself—that is a principle specifically
for those who love themselves.*

PTAHHATP,
Tenth Teaching

WHEN MY SON was five years old he asked me, 'Do you know what I sometimes wonder? I wonder why there is this world.' Of course, this is exactly the sort of thing a child might wonder about but an adult would take for granted. Each morning we wake up and fail to marvel at the fact that we are here—still less, that there is 'here' at all. If we ask 'why is the sky still blue?' or 'what are you saying?' or 'why do you hate me?', there is pause for thought simply in the fact that we can ask such questions. These are not problems in logic or physics but they arise in an impulse to make sense of our lives. We have no reason to suppose that other animals do the same, but we are faced all around— at the edges of the universe, in the smallest structures of matter, in the basic functions of living cells—with things that do make sense or, we feel certain, must make sense. The fact of meaning is spun through the fabric of this world, and there were Egyptians in ancient times who offered explanations for why the world exists and why things happen here. The ancient Egyptian account of physics discussed in this chapter helps explain many of Ptahhatp's fundamental beliefs about the world that otherwise may seem wholly alien to us, such as his convictions that a divine creator provides a specific reason for each thing that happens, that meaning comes before reality and that our spirits are shared with others in the moment. Still, as perhaps we tend to do with any culture that is not modern and/or Western, we dismiss these ancient accounts as myths about the gods: charming, fanciful, risible perhaps, factually incorrect for sure and, above all, primitive.

For example, while writing this chapter I happened to listen to a series of podcasts in which a learned priest was discussing the modern relevance of paganism. He noted that in all religions 'there are elements of goodness, truth and beauty' and that the myths of other cultures are stories intended 'to tell and to teach deep and meaningful truths'.[1] On the other hand, he noted, the myths of some cultures are 'stupid, they are so outrageous—some of the Egyptian myths of creation and so forth are just weird'.[2] On a different podcast another articulate author insisted that 'there is the death penalty in [pharaonic] Egypt if you kill a frog'.[3] That learned and charitable minds should have been so misled by the presentation of ancient beliefs in modern scholarship is perhaps not surprising: we may wonder whether any Egyptologists take pharaonic religion seriously, working as we do within a culture that presumes the intellectual superiority of modernity, the inevitability of progress as a function of human existence, and frequently relies on reductionist academic doctrines such as structuralism—to wit, that all human intellectual output is the same, once we ignore the differences. By reasoning like this, we establish a priori that we know more about the ancients in our terms than they knew about themselves in their own terms and, after all, there is 'a vast difference between the vocabularies available to a Nietzsche or a Foucault as opposed to a Ptahhotep'[4]—though anybody who has read all three may well consider whether a modern writer is actually able to *say* more using more words in German or French than an ancient writer could say in Ancient Egyptian. Certainly the finest poets say more with less.

One Egyptologist recently commented on the condescensions of our immediate forebears, such as Thomas Young and Sir Alan Gardiner, especially with regard to the fact that so many inscriptions are about rituals and offerings, and concluded not that their attitudes have gone away but,

> The reason that such evaluations today are mostly found in works for wider readerships, such as museum catalogues or other presentations for an interdisciplinary audience, has more to do with Egyptological decorum, where direct denigration of the people studied is usually not regarded as fitting within strictly academic discourse, and perhaps also with the fact that the core focus of the discipline of Egyptology has come to be much more firmly entrenched than it was in Gardiner's day, thus needing less affirmation.[5]

In other words, our modernity (which defines us) and the relatively primitive nature of the ancients (which defines them) may simply be taken for granted in the twenty-first century, with no need for comment —thereby avoiding the awkwardness of openly belittling the intellectual development of a specific group of non-Western people. Every human community has its myths, of course, which feed into common identities, and the community may well understand its myths to be authentic history—this is as true of a modern group of football fans or political activists as it is of a nation. However, what the ancients believed to be their authentic identity is easily reduced by modern opinion to totemistic stories formed in a primal soup of simplistic beliefs about frogs and suchlike; and 'because ancient Egyptian religion is so remote to us there is a danger that it may be analysed as a kind of a fairy-tale or at least ... as purely metaphorical'.[6] Of course, for many of us in the West today the difficulty is to take any religion seriously: if I were to reveal that I am a religious person, this may well affect your opinion of me as an Egyptologist, for better or worse. On the other hand, if I were to reveal that I worship Osiris, this would lead you to question my sanity. I do not, by the way, but there are millions of people alive today who do venerate divine monarchs and/or are devoted to the spirits of ancestors, so how are we to be charitable about our fellow human beings and their inconveniently 'old-fashioned' beliefs—and not just look the other way?

The fact of creation—the fact that 'there is this world'—provides a case in point, especially when we consider Ptahhatp's insistence that whatever happens to you in life has a meaningful cause and that you must question this fact. Can we take such convictions seriously or do we just pat him on the head and praise him for being very clever 'for his age'? We could deduce, along with Aristotle, Sir Isaac Newton and Lord Bertrand Russell, that the created universe must have always existed because otherwise—as only a child may think to ask—where did it come from and why? We could also deduce that everything that happens at bottom is random, unformed and purposeless because how could it not be? If creation were genuinely subject to physical or metaphysical laws, rather than just giving that appearance, then creation itself did not create the laws—be both subject and ruler, as it were—so, again, where did the laws come from and why? There simply must have always been what there is now and, as Lord Russell famously concluded, 'it is illegitimate even to ask the question of the cause of the world'.[7] Nevertheless, Ptahhatp's account of human experience presupposes not only that things happen but that they do so for a reason: therefore—as we surely agree—it does make sense to ask questions, even the question about the original cause of everything. It seems to have become a truism in our own culture that faith equates to belief without evidence, but surely faith is actually a commitment to the reality of meaning in the light of evidence? In the act of asking a question what is required first of all, as a child already knows, is faith that things make sense: a question need not presuppose anything about the answer except that there could be an answer.

That said, of course, the kinds of questions we ask presuppose how we understand reality. As one informed reader of very ancient pharaonic religious texts has noted, 'religious language is usually understood as purely metaphorical'.[8] This modern position is intended to imply that religious texts in any culture can somehow evoke insights, feelings or emotions but the individual words in a religious text are not about anything substantive or real because religion itself does not deal with facts as such—only with insights, feelings and emotions. Of course, this position is quite true, but only insofar as 'all language about things other than physical objects is necessarily metaphorical'.[9] Words do not label things in the manner of the sticky notes on boxes in a removal van, otherwise we could not take the bus home without committing a robbery —and, after all, what is home except where the heart is? Philosophers, scientists and ancient priests alike can be more or less precise in writing, more or less prosaic, more or less interesting, but they cannot be more or less figurative. Are words such as creation, space, mind and home merely metaphors? Not for John the Evangelist, author of perhaps the most famous religious statement in modern Western culture: ἐν ἀρχῇ ἦν ὁ λόγος καὶ ὁ λόγος ἦν πρὸς τὸν θεόν καὶ θεὸς ἦν ὁ λόγος. I am neither a theologian nor a Greek scholar but I understand this to mean 'in the beginning there was Meaning and Meaning was present with God and God was the meaning'. Perhaps we could dispute the 'literal' status of the phrase 'present with God' but, in John's statement, the words God (*Theos*) and Meaning (*ho-logos*) are not figurative; you can argue against the reality of either but not simply dismiss the words themselves as hollow metaphors. Both ideas have been at the heart of Western philosophy as much as Western religion since classical times. Indeed, but what about *before* the ancient Greeks?

Ptahhatp, as we have noted, says the same thing as John the Evangelist: that meaning is not simply an integral aspect of creation, it is prior to physical creation. There is a reason for the existence of every 'thing' or, to put this another way, every 'thing' has a cause. Likewise, meaning is so integral to the human condition that 'it's the measure of humanity: well lived, then in poetry does humanity dwell on this earth'.[10] Specifically, language is an inseparable, indivisible aspect of human existence together, because to suppose that each of us may possess language individually is like supposing that the person who invented the first telephone patiently waited for someone else to invent a second telephone.[11] We can talk to ourselves, of course, but that is still an audience of one. The linguistic reality of human existence speaks to the fact that human beings, innately, are part of a meaningful world and part of a community where we share ourselves, as Ptahhatp insists, if only because we are users of language.

The Shabaka Stone

The simple fact of a meaningful creation brings us to the ancient account of physics according to which a creator—which is divine and, therefore, external to the minds of human beings—stands as the consistent source of intention that provides the reason for each thing or each event, which in turn causes its existence. Ancient Egyptian accounts of creation take many forms but the paradigmatic account of the relationship between words, meaning and creation is to be found in the British Museum among a group of texts inscribed on a single monument known today as the Shabaka Stone after the king who had it commissioned.[12] This decent-sized slab of green breccia from the Wadi Hammamat[13] came to Britain as ballast in a ship from Alexandria, and was bought for the Museum in 1805 by George, 2nd Earl Spencer and future Home Secretary (plate XXI). Across its surface are two lines and sixty-two columns of hieroglyphs 'most elegantly but delicately engraved'[14] — and, sadly, as a result often damaged and in places entirely erased by the Stone's later use in Alexandria, probably as a column base.[15]

However, before we discuss the content itself we have to address the fact that the Shabaka Stone also stands as a model of how an ancient text can be conveniently glossed over without openly denigrating the intellect of its authors simply by denigrating the monument itself — by shooting the messenger, as it were. In this case, the Shabaka Stone's value as a historical source has conveniently been blackened by the use of that darkest of terms — propaganda. Hence, according to the British Museum, the Stone

> purports to be a copy of an ancient worm-eaten document which the pharaoh ordered to be transcribed for posterity, and the compiler of the text has reproduced the layout of early documents and introduced a number of archaic spellings and grammatical usages to lend the piece an air of antiquity. In fact, it is now generally accepted that the text in its present form was composed in Shabaka's own time, and that the story of the rescue of the papyrus is an example of a rhetorical device well known in Egyptian royal inscriptions and should not be accepted as a piece of genuine history.[16]

Accordingly, the very institution that holds this ancient treasure asserts that 'the stone was intended as a piece of propaganda' because 'Shabaka was probably seeking to pacify and conciliate the inhabitants and gain the support of the powerful Memphite priesthood'. The last phrase is especially telling because it reduces not only the Stone itself but the king, the priests and the ordinary people, who ostensibly stood behind its words, to no more than base political organisms.

What are we to make of such a dismissal? After all, the term propaganda is surely less appropriate to arcane, mythical inscriptions originally concealed in the darkness of ancient shrines than to political shenanigans in the twentieth century, which is when various distinguished scholars first reached this conclusion.[17] In any event, where would such sceptical claims lead us to? One commentator has even suggested that the Stone was inscribed many centuries later still, and that the attribution to King Shabaka is the actual political conceit![18] On the other hand, as we discussed in Chapter 2, the argument that 'archaic spellings and grammatical usages ... lend the piece an air of antiquity' could just as easily be turned around to argue in favour of the editorial update of a more ancient text — as ancient as prehistory according to certain other commentators.[19] In truth, therefore, the dating of the text on the Shabaka Stone is not at all 'generally accepted' by scholars — it is generally 'disputed'.[20] Indeed, the monument itself was made at a time in Egyptian history when 'artefacts are frequently dated on chronological and genealogical assumptions, and circular arguments'.[21] Even if it were devised by Shabaka for some crude political purpose, was the inscription spun out of thin air and handed to the priests together with the terms of 'an offer they could not refuse' (see page 180)? Is some speculative cloud of dark suspicion over Shabaka's motives sufficient cause to disparage the inscription itself as detritus from a 'game of thrones'?

First of all, we may note that the original home of the Shabaka Stone, the temple of Ptah at Memphis (plate xx), was once so closely identified with the nation as a whole that its ancient name — pronounced something like *ḥo-ku'-ptaḥ* ('enclosure of the spirit of Ptah') — may plausibly be the origin of the Western name for the whole country: *ḥoku'ptaḥ* becomes Greek *Aigupto*, which in turn gives us Egypt in English (as opposed to Misr, the name of the country used by the people of Egypt today, which can be traced back in use to ancient Mesopotamia). During the twentieth century the Shabaka Stone used to be displayed in the same gallery of the British Museum as a decorated wall from the tomb of Ptahshepses, one of the priests mentioned in Chapter 2. In fact, Ptahshepses was High Priest of Ptah in the temple at Memphis during the early Fifth Dynasty and, as such, carried the titles 'elder of the enclosure of Ptah', 'prophet of Ptah and prophet of Sokar in all his places', 'prophet of Hathor in the same places', 'prophet of Truth in the same places' and 'prophet' in at least eight smaller temples; while his duties extended to the king's pyramid complex and to three vast sun-temples nearby, which are among the mere handful of monuments of Fifth Dynasty kings still surviving. Ptahshepses was also termed 'great-

Fragment of a larger than life-sized statue of Taharqa, best attested pharaoh of the Twenty-fifth Dynasty. His Assyrian enemies and most modern narratives identify him, first and foremost, as 'black'. Granite. 35 cm (1 ft 1¾ in.) high. Karnak.

est of directors of artists', a title common to every High Priest of Ptah throughout history,[22] and one that suggests the reciprocal flow of inspiration and thanksgiving from creator-god through his chief celebrant to, and from, the temple's artisans. Henceforth, the priests and the temple of Ptah remained at the heart of religious and cultural life to the extent that one marker of the 'end' of pharaonic Egypt is arguably the abolition of the office of High Priest at Memphis in the aftermath of the nation's subjugation by Roman armies. As a consequence of that turn of events, a man named Psherptah (90–41 BC), his ill-fated son Imhotep-Pedubast

(46–30 BC) and lastly his brother-in-law Pisheramun (date of death ominously unknown) would be the last people ever to hold the proud office, perhaps 2,500 years after Ptahshepses had done so.[23]

So, how has the long, monumental history of the temple of Ptah been hijacked by a speculative comment about Shabaka's motives? Why would anyone credit the suggestion that the priests and proud population of Memphis allowed him to purchase their support in exchange for a blatant lie? Part of the answer, as we have discussed, is precisely that the Stone is irremediably ancient and therefore what the inscription actually says is bound to be inconsequential in itself—beyond whatever we feel it adds to our own historical narrative. However, another part of the answer is that Shabaka (r. c. 705–690 BC) belongs to the Twenty-fifth Dynasty and, in modern scholarship, the crux of the prevailing narrative about the Twenty-fifth Dynasty is its foreignness—its hostile invasion of Egypt.[24] Shabaka and his family have become the 'Black Pharaohs' from Kush and the 'fundamental basis of Kushite rule was military power'.[25] Now, the fact that this was a dark-skinned family seems undeniable: in 671 BC the Assyrian ruler Esarhaddon sacked Memphis and overran the palace of Shabaka's successor, Taharqa (r. c. 690–664 BC), where, he noted, 'I found his wives, sons and daughters, who like him had skin as black as tar'.[26] However, the presumption that the kings of the Twenty-fifth Dynasty were black and therefore *foreign*, *militaristic* conquerors is a more insidious line of thinking and one that stands between us and taking the Shabaka Stone seriously—so let us take a brief look at their supposed 'invasion'.

The 'Black Pharaohs'

The practice of organizing Egypt's history by reference to its kings stems from an indigenous tradition, which stretches further back in time than even the Palermo Stone (see page 69); while the practice of grouping kings into dynasties derives from a history written by Manetho, a priest from the Nile Delta, early in the third century BC. On the other hand, the business of dividing Egypt's history into eras or chunks, each with its own defining characteristics, is a wholly modern exercise (see page 17).[27] For instance, all the kings from the Twenty-first Dynasty until the Twenty-fifth Dynasty, including Shabaka, are grouped into what we now term the Third Intermediate Period because 'the most characteristic feature of Egypt during the Third Intermediate Period is the political fragmentation of the country'.[28] Specifically, this chunk of history is supposedly characterized by: 'the distinct North–South divide' in Egypt along ethnic lines;[29] the destabilizing impact of the different ethnic groups on indigenous Egyptian culture;[30] the hostile invasion of Egypt from the Nubian kingdom of Kush; and — most definitively of all, it would seem — the confusion and 'numerous unresolved problems'[31] still apparent in our attempts to make sense of this period.

We can at least be sure that the event defining the end of the New Kingdom and the beginning of the Third Intermediate Period was the loss of the Nubian lands of Wawat and Kush from Egyptian control during the eleventh century BC. As it happens, this was the consequence of a civil war during which the viceroy of Nubia, Panehsy, became entangled in a dispute about the royal succession — a dispute that created a rift in the family of King Ramesses XI that lasted for a generation after his death. Panehsy himself had been one of the three most senior officials in Ramesses' palace and 'was, apparently, loyal to the end',[32] so explanations for the loss of Nubia based on anti-Egyptian nationalism are speculative at best. Nevertheless, losing Nubia after more than 400 years as an integral aspect of the Egyptian state was transformative: not only does civil war indicate extreme dysfunction within the Egyptian regime, the turn of events seemingly set Nubia and Egypt on separate historical paths. Then suddenly, more than 300 years later, in the eighth century BC — or late in the Twenty-second Dynasty in those terms — a Nubian king named Piye (r. c. 750–720 BC) erected a stela in far-distant Kush recording his great procession to receive homage from four kings and five other named power-brokers in the Delta and Faiyum regions of Egypt. Egypt was once again in the grip of civil war, and Piye's account casts a retrospective shadow across the entire Third Intermediate Period. To begin, there is civil war and the loss of Nubia; at the end, there is a fractured kingship and such political turmoil that Nubian armies are able to march the length of Egypt. How could we suppose anything except that civil war had brought Egypt to the brink of collapse and subjugation by hostile, foreign, militaristic invaders?

In reality, what happened in Nubia in the three centuries after Wawat and Kush were lost from Egyptian rule is so obscured by a dearth of archaeological and textual evidence that this period is often referred to as the Nubian Dark Age. To be clear, we cannot trace Piye's line back further than a generation before him and even the line of succession of its best-known kings, from Piye through Shabaka to Taharqa, is still up for discussion.[33] Indeed, before Piye's stela was first discovered in Kush, about 1862, no one even suspected his existence, so whatever cultural and hereditary descent there might have been from Panehsy or Ramesses XI to Piye's family is lost in the darkness. Then again, to put this another way, what we do know about the Twenty-fifth Dynasty is that when they first appear in the pages of history they are thoroughly immersed in the pharaonic ruling culture of Egypt and active there in the south as much as they are active in Nubia. Moreover, whereas standard histories of the Third Intermediate Period concentrate on a definitive division between northern and southern lines of kings in Egypt, Piye's account indicates that the political fractures in his time actually ran exclusively throughout the north. More to the point, when he brought his armies to Egypt, almost the entire Nile Valley, in Egypt as well as Nubia, was or had recently been subject to Piye—and there is much to notice in this.

Both the Old Testament and the Assyrian rulers recognized the Twenty-fifth Dynasty as the rulers of two countries, Egypt (which they call Mizraim or Musr) and Kush; and the kings are often depicted on their monuments with a pair of cobras fronting their crowns to symbolize kingship in two lands. In 664 BC Tanwatiamuni succeeded as king in this line and erected a stela, alongside that of Piye, in which he offers an insight into the symbolism of the cobras:

Hormakhet, a son of Shabaka, served as High Priest of Amun-Ra at Thebes into the reign of Tanwatiamuni. His name is unequivocally Egyptian, as is the style of his statue. Quartzite. 66 cm (2 ft 2 in.) high. Twenty-fifth Dynasty. Karnak.

The year of his arising as king ... his person saw a dream in the night: two snakes, one in his right hand, the other in his left. His person woke up but could not understand it, and <therefore> said, 'Why would this happen to me?' So he was answered, 'You have the Valley: seize the Delta! The Twin Ladies have appeared from your brow since the earth has been given to you in its length and breadth. No one else should divide it with you.'[34]

In other words, Tanwatiamuni's dream indicates that the cobras were a symbol of the Nile Valley and the Nile Delta together; and that Upper Egypt as much as Nubia formed the Valley loyal to him. The biblical and Assyrian perspective on both Egypt/Musr (that is, the Nile Delta as far as Memphis) and Kush (that is, the Nile Valley) is a view of the same political geography but seen from Mesopotamia, not Africa. Accordingly, we must not downplay the fact that Piye's stela actually presents us with a statement about subduing a *rebellion* against him among the rulers in the Nile Delta, and about bringing former supporters back to his side — foremost among them being Peftjawawybast, king of the Egyptian city of Heracleopolis and formerly High Priest of Ptah at Memphis.[35] Indeed, Piye begins his campaign not by massing Nubian armies for an invasion at the border of Egypt but by celebrating the New Year at Thebes and joining his (Egyptian?) troops near Heracleopolis, from where he leads them to Memphis, Heliopolis and the Delta to obtain promises of loyalty from the 'other' kings there.

In other words, the presumption that Shabaka's 'black' dynasty was exclusively 'Kushite' and had its genesis in a cultural realm distinct from Upper Egypt is chauvinism, belied by the fact that we know so little about its origins. When these people first emerge as kings they do so to write, rule, worship and be buried in pharaonic style — in fact, in a most traditional form. Shabaka, for example, took Neferkara, the throne name of King Pepy II of the Old Kingdom, for his own throne name. Like the Shabaka Stone itself, the monumental inscriptions that survive from the Twenty-fifth Dynasty are written in the Ancient Egyptian language (plate XXIII). The major temples of these kings, whether in Nubia or in Egypt, were developed alongside, or as part of, much older

Temple shrine, decorated with a scene showing Shabaka purifying
a statue of Osiris of Abydos, the ancient god of Egyptian kingship.
Granite. 1.27 m (4 ft 2 in.) high. Twenty-fifth Dynasty. Esna.

pharaonic temples—including the temples of Napata, where the stelae
of Piye and Tanwatiamuni were discovered. From Shabaka's generation, if not earlier, various queens and other senior members of the
royal household were buried at Abydos in Egypt, beside the processional route to the tombs of Aha, Den, Qaʻa and the earliest pharaohs.
Even the kings' own pyramids at al-Kurru in Kush all too obviously
hark back to the royal burial practices of Izezi and the Old Kingdom
(plate XXII). In fact, George Reisner (1867–1942), the first excavator
of al-Kurru, went so far as to argue that the cemeteries here exemplify
the evolution of an indigenous Nubian pharaonic culture, emulating
the course of evolution in Egypt albeit more than 2,000 years later—an
interpretation that has not entirely gone away.[36] Of course, rather than
insisting that a mindless evolutionary process somehow reinvented the
wheel in 'black' Africa, it is far simpler to conclude that the kings buried

at al-Kurru felt themselves to be part of the pharaonic heritage as much as the other kings in Egypt at this time. No doubt, of course, different areas of Shabaka's realm had their own distinct cultures or languages, and many of his subjects did not identify themselves as Egyptians—but for many (most?) of them, Egypt was their place of birth and their home (see page 175). However, the point here is not about identity but about kingship: did it really mean something intrinsically different to rule as a 'Black Pharaoh' in Kush than it did in Upper Egypt? Is it so difficult to believe that Shabaka would have had more interest in the ancient texts of the Temple of Ptah than base political convenience?

There is a final point to notice here, because we gain a different perspective by recognizing that the Third Intermediate Period was not simply an era of 'political fragmentation'. For instance, Shoshenq I (r. *c.* 945–925 BC), founder of the Twenty-second Dynasty, led a major military campaign in the Near East, recorded in a monumental inscription on the walls of the temple of Amun-Ra at Karnak (see page 34). In its own terms, this campaign took place on a grand scale, and today it is conventionally identified with a vast African army of Egyptians, Libyans and Nubians with 1,200 chariots and 60,000 horsemen mentioned in the Old Testament.[37] Shoshenq's Egypt, it seems, was far from politically reduced and divided. Indeed, if we look at how modern historians describe the Twenty-second Dynasty, we notice considerable agreement about what happens at the beginning; but, by the end, even our understanding of the line of succession is frankly a mess.[38] If we then look at how scholars reconstruct the Twenty-third Dynasty, there is wholesale disagreement; there is obvious confusion with whatever is being said more generally about the messy end of the Twenty-second Dynasty; and there is minimal correspondence with Manetho's original dynastic list. In other words, we can wonder how much we truly know about this period—or, to put this another way, whether it constitutes an Egyptian 'Dark Age'. At this point, we are obliged to refer to a contemporary inscription in the Temple at Karnak, where the High Priest Osorkon records how a 'furious storm occurred in this land' during the reign of his father, king Takeloti II (who may or may not belong to either the Twenty-second or the Twenty-third Dynasty[39]), following which 'war took hold in the north and south' and 'years passed in confrontation, each seizing his neighbour without taking thought for his own son and protecting whoever had been born to him'. Although a historian would presumably hope to connect this bitter conflict to other shadowy events at Thebes, the problem remains that we know so very little of substance about this civil breakdown and these murderous reprisals among local communities. More to the point, this is a whole century before Piye's campaign and he, in turn, makes no mention whatsoever of political violence at Thebes. So, in the end, we are left with two crucial facts: that during the late 800s BC the throne of Egypt became increasingly divided, mostly between branches of the same royal family, and this division proliferated most keenly and persisted longest in the Delta; and that, at some indeterminate moment during the following century—a century every bit as 'dark' in Egypt as in Nubia—the Twenty-fifth Dynasty of pharaohs became established throughout the relatively stable (in political terms) Nile Valley. Nevertheless, when we discuss the Twenty-fifth Dynasty today, Egyptologists are not inclined to talk about an Egyptian 'Dark Age', whereas the Nubian Dark Age has become a commonplace. Perhaps it remains too convenient (or too seductive) to imagine that the 'Black Pharaohs' simply rode into Egypt out of the heart of darkness?

The physics of meaning

Though we have been obliged to address the dubious argument used to discredit the Shabaka Stone, the point of the foregoing discussion is that the dating and the purpose of the actual monument are irrelevant to us here. The content of an inscription that we can call here *Why Things Happen* is what matters, and this is consistent with the oldest religious texts from Egypt in terms of both the language and the ideas that underpin this so-called Memphite theology.[40] Its account of creation, even in the form given to us on the Shabaka Stone, certainly predates the earliest accounts of creation in the Western tradition, whether from the Old Testament in the Hebrew written tradition or, for example, from Democritus in

Detail of Shabaka's royal titulary on the Shabaka Stone. His personal name, in the left-hand cartouche, has been erased at a later date but evidently the monument, with his putative propaganda, was otherwise left intact.

the classical tradition—neither of which it agrees with, either in broad terms or in points of detail. Interestingly, however, *Why Things Happen* does bear comparison with the basic arguments of some early Greek philosophers, such as Anaximander of Miletus, who postdate Shabaka by a couple of centuries—and the temple of Ptah by a couple of millennia.[41] Perhaps this allows the possibility that pre-Socratic Greek philosophers were not purely the products of indigenous European thought but, like King Shabaka, grew up in a world where the philosophical ideas of 'pre-scientific', 'pre-logical' Egypt were familiar? That is as may be but, for now, let us take a look at what the inscription talks about.

At the top of the Shabaka Stone a single line gives the king's name and titles in a balanced composition reading in both directions from the centre. Beneath this, another line explains the project Shabaka has commissioned—the very line that led to the monument's integrity being so severely questioned during the last century:

> Consecrating once more, by his person, the very writing from the estate of his father, Ptah South-Of-His-Wall. For his person found worm-eaten what the ancients had made, so it cannot be read from beginning to end. Therefore, [his person has consecrated it] once

more, better than it ever has been, in the hope that his name will remain because his monument will have endured in the estate of his father, Ptah South-Of-His-Wall, throughout time—being what the son of the sun [Shabaka] has made for his father, Ptah Risen-Land, in order that he (= the king) may act given life for all time.

At this point, we should probably note that images of Shabaka and his officials often incorporate a distinctive physiognomy, with robust limbs and torsos and square, broad-nosed faces. This has often been termed the 'Kushite' style and, of course, a lazy, crude assumption has tended to explain this by reference to the subjects' 'black' physiognomy in life. More recent studies, however, indicate that the style is based on the awareness of much older art, especially of Old Kingdom statues. Indeed, we find the same style used elsewhere in Egypt at this time and it might well have developed originally in the north, where so many of the most ancient models were to be found in the pyramid fields of Saqqara, Giza and so on.[42] Accordingly, Egyptologists now tend to acknowledge that 'throughout the period there is also a growing awareness and harking back to the past', which is the genuine explanation for this distinctive style.[43] Perhaps the key to making sense of Shabaka's 'propaganda'— not just in the Temple of Ptah but in his rebuilding work in temples elsewhere, such as those at Esna, Luxor, Karnak and Dendera[44]—was his intention to stabilize the foundations of an ancient nation that had recently become worm-eaten and rotten.[45]

Beneath these top lines, the remainder of the inscription takes up sixty-one columns, reading from left to right across a single face of the Stone but written in the retrograde manner typically used for copying out the most formal religious texts.[46] By retrograde we mean the hiero-glyphic signs in each column are turned round in relation to the direction of reading, as though the English translation were to be written like this:

Column 4	Column 3	Column 2	Column 1
←	←	←	←
which is what allows all perception.	smell, and they may ascend to the mind,	see, the ears may hear and the nose may	Gods have been born that the eyes may

Evidently, to generate the hieroglyphic inscription several texts have been copied out together, distinguished from one another by the use of dividing lines and headings, and presumably taken from more than one source. That said, according to the way they are arranged as well as their content, the various texts clearly form complementary groups. Interestingly, not every column is completely filled with text, which is not what we expect of a hieroglyphic inscription, though the same layout may be seen in hieratic technical books such as the Rhind Mathematical Papyrus; in several instances, the writing comes to a natural stop short of the end of a column, perhaps just because it has been laid out beside a longer complementary text. However, the overall arrangement of texts across the monument is badly obscured by the almost complete loss of writing in the twenty-nine columns in the middle. The inscription as it survives today effectively divides into a left-hand section and a right-hand section, and we find *Why Things Happen* on the right—in other words, at the end of the Shabaka Stone.

However, what drew Shabaka's interest to these various texts may be best explained by those on the left, which have long been recognized as the record or 'script' of a dramatic performance—possibly, it seems to me, of the coronation ceremony or installation of the king at Memphis, with attendant speeches given at appropriate moments in the unfolding drama. In fact, the very beginning is lost and only tantalizing snippets remain, such as 'generating it by the Non-being which has given birth to the Nine'. The term 'Non-being' or 'Who is without being' (*atmu* in Ancient Egyptian) refers to the source of all creation, which must be real and present without 'being' because the very possibility of anything 'being' depends upon it. Remember the child's question? If the universe was created in a first moment, where did it come from? In these terms, whatever there is came from nothing, or from 'Non-being', as we shall see.

The Nine, who also appear frequently in the text, are the first, divine creatures: Ptah Tatjenen, Shu, Tefenet, Geb, Nut, Osiris, Isis, Seth and Nephthys. Accordingly, the narrative does seem mythological and 'weird' until we appreciate that these names have meanings and associations: Ptah Tatjenen is literally the Risen Earth, the origin or potential form of creation; Shu and Tefenet, respectively the words for energy (or light) and matter, are the elements of creation whose interaction gives rise to the World below (Geb) and the Sky above (Nut) as the three-dimensional space we now inhabit (plate XIX). Osiris, Isis, Seth and Nephthys are the first inhabitants of the World and the Sky. In other words, the number Nine derives from the sequence: totality (Tatjenen), distinguishable elements (energy/matter), distinct forms (earth/sky, male/female) and the original inhabitants of the World (two pairs of male and female, Osiris with Isis and Seth with Nephthys).

The first inhabitant is Osiris, who had two defining characteristics: he was a king and he was mortal. The counter-intuitive appearance of a king before there is anyone to rule emphasizes that life itself is governed by elemental principles, such as the principles of physics, mathematics and justice—which, therefore, humanity did not subsequently invent. Nevertheless, Osiris was murdered and butchered by his unruly and ambitious brother, Seth. Isis bound Osiris' fractured body in linen, buried him as a king at Abydos, and breathed the next life into him. Death was doubly defeated when she conceived his son, Horus, and the template for the legitimate transfer of royal authority was set at the beginning of the World. In time, Horus grew up to vanquish Seth and reconcile to his rule whatever violence or rebellion seeks to transgress the elemental principles of the World. In historical terms, each and every pharaoh down to Shabaka stood in this line of succession.

The texts in columns 10–12 are intact and pick up with this narrative. First, Horus is given the marshes and Seth the grasses, and the World (Geb) says to them 'I have separated you'. Meanwhile, the dramatic narrative is addressed to us:

col. 10 According to the World's intention it is bad that Horus' portion is the same as Seth's portion. col. 11 It was the World that gave the father's inheritance to Horus because he is the son col. 12 of his own first-born.

The end of this section would seem to be the actual coronation, as the World tells the Nine, 'I have commanded, "One alone!" All this belongs to the heir, to the son of my first-born son. He is a son born of me.' Next, he says to Horus, 'You are the eldest son. One alone and heir; one alone and my heir.' Finally, Horus is proclaimed as the king in whom Ptah Risen-Earth (the original creation) has been restored as intended by Ptah South-Of-His-Wall (the creator):

> [col. 13] Horus stands on the earth. United now is this earth that had been proclaimed in the royal name 'The Risen Earth of South-Of-His-Wall that possesses time'. [col. 14] The twin crowns named 'Great of Control' have sprouted from his head. So is he Horus, who has appeared as hereditary and sovereign king and united the Twin Lands from Memphis, from the place where the Twin Lands are joined. [col. 15] Whereupon a linen string and a papyrus stalk have been placed on the doors of the Ptah Temple. They are Horus and Seth contented. They are joined so that there should be no quarrelling between them [col. 16] in the places where they ... ... having been united in the Ptah Temple as the seat of the Twin Lands, where grass-land and marsh-land are raised.

So Memphis ('where the Twin Lands are joined'), more specifically the Ptah Temple, is presented as the origin of creation—the risen earth 'that

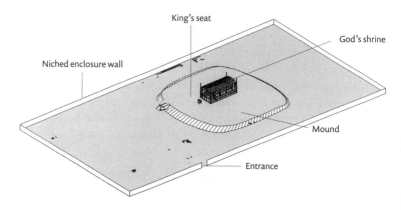

Plan of the early temple of Horus at Hieraconpolis, which is both the model for the Step Pyramid outside Memphis and a representation of the 'Risen Earth' as the site of creation described in the Shabaka Stone.

Retrograde writing forms the heading to *Why Things Happen*:
read left to right, 'The gods have happened out of Ptah';
read right to left, 'Ptah is the being of the gods'.

possesses time'; and Horus, king by birth and now king by fact, stands
here while his legitimate authority embraces the inherently destructive
and disruptive ambitions of change, in the form of his murderous uncle
Seth. Sadly, the rest of this drama is lost but the remaining traces suggest
there might have been one or two versions of the story of Osiris' death,
a story which also appears below.

On the right of the Shabaka Stone, the specific text of *Why Things
Happen* begins with both a heading and an introduction, written across
four columns. At this point the retrograde writing of the inscription is
most relevant because, like Ptahhatp's name, the heading can be read
forwards and backwards. Read in the direction of the text it says 'the
gods have happened out of Ptah', whereas read in the opposite direction—the direction the retrograde hieroglyphs face—it says 'Ptah is the
being of the gods'. In other words, read one way it is a statement about
how the gods have come to be from the creator, and read the other
way a statement about how their continued existence depends on the
creator, and these turn out to be two themes in what follows. Beneath
this heading, by way of the introduction, Ptah is named four times:

I. *Ptah on the great seat.* Seated on a throne at the origin of creation,
Ptah is definitively the ruler—an image also forging a tangible link
between this text and the previous drama of the installation of the
king at Memphis.

II. *Ptah of potential, father of Non-being.* Now identified with the
simple possibility of creation, Ptah is the seed for creation out of what
is otherwise nothing (see page 187).

III. *Ptah Nekhbet, mother who gave birth to Non-being.* By assuming the name of Nekhbet—the goddess associated with the most ancient temple of the living king, Horus—Ptah becomes the 'mother' in whom creation takes place.

IV. *Ptah, most important, who is the heart and tongue of the Nine.* Ultimately, Ptah is meaning (heart) and form (tongue) for the first, divine creatures. This will now be the model for the account of creation which follows, and we may perhaps recall the ideal in Ptahhatp's First Conclusion: to learn truth from experience and from those who have already learned from experience, and so think and speak accordingly.

Why Things Happen itself begins at the top of a new column next to the heading, and seems complete as we have it:

col. 53 Happening from the heart is an expression of Non-being; happening from the tongue is an expression of Non-being. Ptah, the most important, has been made perfect in all the gods and their spirits. For from this heart and from this tongue, col. 54 from it Horus has happened out of Ptah and from it Thoth has happened out of Ptah.

So, creation comes into being out of Non-being through the intention of the creator expressed as a word. As we have discussed—and as Ptahhatp assumes—all things that happen have an intrinsic meaning and form because they are first of all a thought and then a word expressed in language (see page 191). The first elements of creation are divine—not only the gods but also their spirits, which in turn entail relationships in accordance with Ptahhatp's Seventh Teaching. Creation immediately assumes both the principle of elemental laws, embodied in Horus the king, and the principle of knowing or understanding them, embodied in Thoth, the god of wisdom and learning (see Foreword). As a child knows, questions make sense because there is reason behind what happens, in accordance with Ptahhatp's Fifth Teaching ('seek the meaning for you in every event'). The constant rediscovery of the same truth by every child is itself proof that meaning is to be found outside the minds of humans, which, nonetheless, are open to knowing and learning. As Ptahhatp's Twenty-sixth Teaching argues, this openness is demonstrated

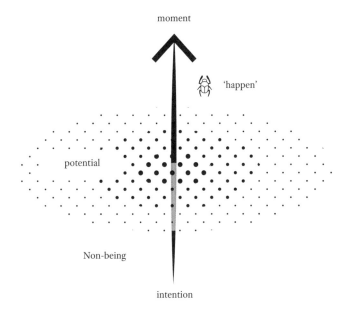

Schematic representation of how any intentions act on potential (energy and matter) to make a moment 🪲 *kheper* 'happen'. According to *Why Things Happen*, it is a divine intention that first makes each moment in time happen out of Non-being, constantly repeating the same process as in the first moment of creation.

most clearly in the meaning that may be found in relationships, which are structured in many ways but always rely on the coming together of individuals ('a spirit may relax with whoever loves it: it is about spirits giving along with God'). The narrative continues as follows:

> Whereupon the tongue presides in accordance with <the fact> that it shall introduce every body and introduce every speech of every god, every person, all flocks and crawling things, and whatever lives thinking and speaking every fact that he wishes, ^{col. 55} and his Nine are before him as the teeth and lips. They are the exclamation that Non-being gives. The Nine of Non-being happen out of his ejaculation and his fingers. Surely the Nine are the teeth and lips in this very

speech which acclaimed the identity of all material and out of which Energy and Matter emerged.

Here, the words 'exclamation' and 'ejaculation' are the same (*metu*) in the original text. In the first phrase, the Nine are the first physical expression of creation from Ptah, in the form of both his mouth as the space in which words happen and the words that come out of it; in its second use, the word-play transforms the creative act into a seminal discharge of potential through masturbation. Still, the meaning of what is created comes first ('presides'), and each physical form finds its unique expression ('identity') in the interaction of Energy and Matter caused by the expression of words (see page 191).

The text then develops the argument that things have meanings and therefore we have minds to learn these meanings and senses to inform our minds, which, at the end of the day, is the essence of what Ptahhatp teaches:

> col. 56 The Nine have been born that the eyes may see, the ears may hear and the nose may smell, and they may ascend to the mind, which is what allows all perception. The tongue it is that relates what the heart has thought. So have all the gods been born that constitute his Nine. Surely, every divine word has happened from what the heart thinks col. 57 and what the tongue commands. So forces act within the limits set down that make all foods and all offerings, and make what is loved and what is hated. So has life been given to one who brings contentment, death has been given to the one who brings discord. So all work, all art, all that arms do, the moving of legs col. 58 and the motion of every body part act according to his command — the speaking of what the heart thinks and what emerges from the tongue — that defines all material.

Creation first brings the gods, which are the divine creatures through whom the creator can experience its creation, and then human awareness and learning follow the divine model (expressed previously as the presence of Thoth). However, even the gods are restricted by the principles of what is allowed or intended — the principles of physics, mathematics, justice and so on. Things happen within the limits of what is intended, and seeking to transgress these limits brings futility and 'death', whereas acceptance ('contentment') brings 'life', which is specifically the point at which Ptahhatp begins his teachings. This awareness is developed still further:

> Whereupon the action of Non-being, which has created the gods to be Ptah, has been spoken. Thus is he the Risen Earth, which has given birth to the gods, from which all material has emerged as offerings and provisions, as ^{col. 59} the offerings for the gods, as every perfected material. So Thoth (wisdom) has recognized that his (Ptah's) strength is greater than all gods. So Ptah is content after his making all material and every divine word. Accordingly, he has given birth to gods, has made cities, has furnished communities, has put the gods in their shrines, ^{col. 60} has made their offerings abundant, has furnished their shrines, has sculpted their images to satisfy their wishes. So have gods come as their images in every wood, every stone, every clay and every material in which he is growing. ^{col. 61} There they have happened. So has he assembled all the gods and their spirits, made content and joined with the one who holds the Twin Lands.

In other words, all creation is from the creator, including human creativity—remember, the High Priest of Ptah was 'greatest of directors of artists'. More to the point, Ptah was not simply the original creator but remains the creator, ever-present in every action. The sculpted images of gods take their meaning from the creative act and from the offerings made 'to satisfy their wishes', but then so do the cities and other human-built communities that surround the temples, as Metjen would attest.

Finally, this super-abundance (a 'divine granary') of creativity is related to death, which may otherwise appear to be the undoing of creation:

> A divine granary of the Risen One is the Great Seat: which brings together the intentions of the gods that are from the Ptah Temple; which possesses what lives, which possesses what is done; on which the Twin Lands live ^{col. 62} because of the fact of Osiris as he drowns in its water, that Isis and Nephthys may be seen as they watch him and are consummated by him. Horus commands Isis 'Do not delay!' and commands Nephthys 'Do not delay!' that they will grab Osiris,

undo his drowning and ^{col. 63} reverse things at the correct moment. So, they bring him to the earth and he passes through secret gateways in the shrines of those who possess eternity to the processional path of rising, in the horizon on the paths of the sun, from the Great Seat. ^{col. 64} He joins with the gathering of officials and fraternizes with the gods of the Risen Earth, which is Ptah who possesses the years. So Osiris comes into being from the earth in the Enclosure of the Elder in the northern half of this very earth to which he came when his son, Horus, appeared as hereditary king and appeared as sovereign king out of the action of his father, Osiris, along with the gods that precede him and those that follow him.

Accordingly, the deceased is returned to the fertile earth not to rot but to pass through the replete, divine darkness of the inundation and rise like the sun as one of the gods, which are now to be found ahead of Ptah on the Great Seat, the site of the original creation. In other words, the deceased is making the mortal journey in reverse and our view of 'death ahead' is literally turned round.

Shabaka and Ptahhatp

According to *Why Things Happen*, meaning is spun through the fabric of creation because the expression of divine thought as divine words is the very means of creating out of Non-being, just as thinking and expression are the only human means available to create out of nothing. Otherwise, our activities in the world, from nuclear physics to art to sexual repro-duction, are so much rearrangement of what has already been made and 'we all live in second-hand suits and there are doubtless atoms in my chin which have served many another man, many a dog, many an eel, many a dinosaur.'[47] On the other hand, if we admit the reality of a creator, or even the fact that creation has happened once—a moment out of time, in which all the energy and matter there ever will be came into being instantaneously—then we cannot rule out the possibility of everything that there is being un-made in an instant. Of course, for each of us this is what death threatens to be, but our own astronomers do allow that

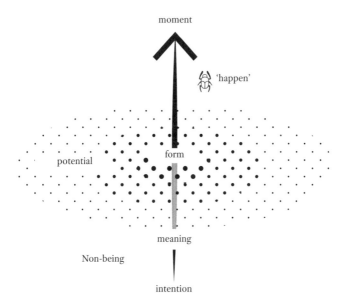

Representation of how the divine intention acts on potential
(energy and matter) specifically by using words to create each moment.
Words give each moment a defined meaning and form before it happens.

even 'the universe has a beginning and an end at singularities that form
a boundary to space-time and at which the principles of science break
down'.[48] In fact, from its inception the modern theory of the 'Big Bang'
has often been resisted precisely because, as the celebrated physicist
Stephen Hawking (1942–2018) summarized, 'many people do not like
the idea that time has a beginning, probably because it smacks of divine
intervention. There has to be some organizing principle.'[49] Evidently,
this is the very inference that some ancient Egyptians drew: since there
is anything rather than nothing, it must have an origin, a cause and the
elemental principles that give it form. The simple observation that any
story has a beginning and an end, a plot and an author who is not part

of the story turns out to be a reiteration of the structure of the most mundane and mind-boggling stories of all—the story of the universe and the story of 'You, here'.

Since classical times, Western philosophy of any persuasion has been driven by a conception of 'being' as though it were a persistent quality of things. However, in pharaonic Egyptian texts, 'being' (*unen*) as a quality (an intrinsic aspect) is true of humans only insofar as they have become 'ideal' or 'perfected' (*nefru*) and provide an enduring example for others, as Ptahhatp notes in his First Conclusion—'if an ideal instance comes about through one who is a master, they are (*unen*) meaningful for eternity'. In fact, the word 'being' (*unen*) is used principally in funerary texts, describing how we will find ourselves in the next life. In *Why Things Happen*, the world present to us here and 'everything that is the case'[50] is a fact because it has *happened*—not because

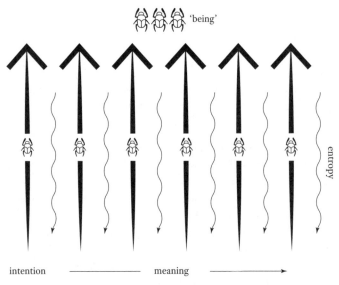

A sequence of distinct 'happenings' brought about individually by a consistent intention has a common meaning and, in that sense alone, has a common persistent 慧慧慧 *khepru* 'being'.

it somehow possesses the quality of 'being' (that is, already exists and will go on doing so). Non-being is real, according to the ancient account, in the sense that Non-being is the origin of everything, just as the origin of a graph is zero; and there is the potential for anything to happen (come into being) within the limits set down by, for instance, physics or mathematics. On the other hand, by definition not-happening does not happen: everything that is the case must happen. Remember, in the Sixth Teaching, Ptahhatp warns you not to worry about what has not happened. So, in this account it is 'happening' that matters, not 'being'. What could this possibly mean? It means, of course, that there is only *now*.

The immediacy of creation in each moment contrasts starkly with a view of creation as a single 'Big Bang' at the beginning of time.[51] In the ancient view, every account of creation is a statement about now. Whereas in Western philosophy we are inclined to see creatures, such as ourselves, as discrete objects or entities that exist independently of one another through time, in *Why Things Happen* we are one point in the constant exclamation of a divine will. The creator's intention brings the present moment into being and in turn produces form through the interaction of Energy and Matter, which are the means of expression — that is, 'the teeth and lips' of the creator form 'the exclamation that Non-being gives'. Any event in which you are involved is in reality a cluster of individual moments given meaning by the persistence of the original intention. Likewise, a creature such as a human being is a cluster or sequence of individual happenings. Accordingly, in the Ancient Egyptian language the fact of 'being' here is more frequently expressed as 'happenings', as we can see in the phrase heading *Why Things Happen* — read in one direction 'the gods have happened out of Ptah' and in the other 'Ptah is the being (literally 'happenings') of the gods' (see page 185). In other words, we are all of us here now from moment to moment rather than 'being' a distinct entity that somehow persists from one moment to the next, despite appearances.

Even a lifetime is a sequence of happenings in which you and everyone else plays a part: as such, there is no 'You' that stands apart from these happenings. A quick glance through your own photographs will reveal how no single 'You' has persisted in a physical sense. The 'You' who began reading this sentence no longer exists (remember the First Conclusion, 'speaking to whoever comes later is the ideal because only they can hear'). With this awareness, think how your expectations, beliefs and values have changed since your earliest childhood memories and you may perhaps recognize that no single 'You' has persisted in a mental sense either. Then consider the fact that your future, and who 'You' are soon going to be, is not already determined (at least, in any way that you are aware of) and you may have some sense that whatever 'You' are does not exist apart from the here and now—as Ptahhatp points out in the Twenty-second Teaching. So, where are 'You'? In your head? Your heart? Your liver? Your genes—or your gonads, as the sociobiologists suggest? Is that 'You' in the mirror? How much of 'You' is actually held in the hearts of others—in your relationships, as Ptahhatp's conception of the 'spirit' insists?

You may have a strong sense of the answer to these questions but you would still do well to appreciate that the finest ancient minds might have answered very differently—as, for instance, Ptahhatp in his Fourteenth Teaching ('great are the thoughts given by God but whoever listens to their appetite belongs to an enemy'). Plato likewise argued that higher human gifts, such as poetry, prophesy, healing and love for another—gifts that may still define people we admire or follow—are literally a 'gift' (*dosis*) because they are obtained through divine inspiration, not from within.[52] According to the pre-eminent psychologist Carl Jung (1875–1961), 'we are so captivated by and entangled in our subjective consciousness that we have forgotten the age-old fact that God speaks chiefly through dreams and visions',[53] as Ptahhatp affirms in his Tenth Teaching ('it was God who made their talent and he coaches them while they sleep'). Of course, many people in many cultures make similar claims about matters such as music and dreams, to the extent that 'inspiration' and 'inspire' (literally 'breathe into someone') have become synonyms for the artistic process, both in terms of how artists obtain ideas and how they lead an audience towards Plato's higher gifts.

To take an analogy, we might laugh at the suggestion that a 'primitive' might believe there are little people inside our television sets. However, an ancient Egyptian might have chuckled at our modern conviction that we all think similar thoughts because we have essentially the same brains: this would seem like concluding that we all see the same television programmes because all our television sets are essentially put together in the same way—with the same little people inside. In fact, we know that we watch the same programmes because they are transmitted from a common source. According to *Why Things Happen*, we are present as a shared moment in space. We are not self-created—we are not even self-possessed, any more than an individual atom is. We belong to the moment and we belong to others. In this conception of

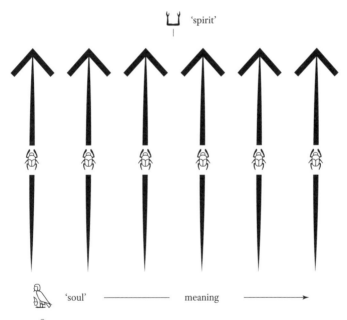

The 𓅢 *ba* 'soul' of each person is one example of how a common meaning manifests through countless individual moments in time ('nows'), each of which is present to others as the person's 𝖴 *ka* 'spirit'.

reality, you are never alone: there is you and the whole universe happening round you.

Likewise, in Ptahhatp's teachings, the instinct to find meaning in events does not ask you to impose your own meaning on whatever happens in your life. Rather, the fact of meaning, the reason for what you do, is already present to be learned in each and every instance of the fact that things have happened when there might as well have been nothing. Without that creative intention there may well be nothing once more. This description of time is more like that provided by quantum physics: each moment arises independently of the moment before as a matter of probability, and intention (or information, as we would say today[54]) is the crucial variable for determining the probability of what happens next. Of course, this does not imply that the ancients understood quantum physics, still less that the descriptive authority of quantum physics in our culture owes anything to the ancients. However, we must be aware that quantum physicists are exploring the limits of modern Western understanding. If we recognize that there are such limits—and what hubris to imagine otherwise—then we need not reduce the ideas of the ancients to crude, primitive prototypes of our own. They are simply not restricted by the same ingrained cultural limits in thinking as our own ideas are—because they have reasoned to different conclusions.

Whereas each moment immediately passes, Ptahhatp's teaching about the relationship between human conduct and a timeless truth emphasizes the permanence of truth and values in our relationships with others. This is a straightforward position but far from simple in its implications. If we follow the argument of *Why Things Happen*, any creature—such as we are—is one aspect of a meaningful cluster of individual happenings characterized by the persistence of a creative intention, not by the persistence of any distinct entity. Without meaningful cause, life is no more than 'earth to earth, ashes to ashes, dust to dust'.[55] As such, we can obviously note that the only surviving copies of *The Teaching of Ptahhatp*, the oldest book in the world, have reached us via tombs. The basis of meaning is the timeless truth that stands apart from humans—the creator that gave cause and meaning to creation, and must stand apart from the universe just as the author is not a character in the book. Ptahhatp (and Kagemni too) identify this creator simply as 'God'. *Why Things Happen* names the creator as Ptah South-Of-His-Wall—the name used at Memphis—whose only necessary characteristic is creating by intention and expression in order to know creation. The same authority is the origin of wisdom and justice because, as Ptahhatp explains, wisdom and justice are knowledge of the creator's elemental principles (what we may call science) and intentions (what we may call philosophy). In other words, accepting that the world is what it is for a reason, and not what you wish it to be, and accepting the radical commitment to learning (in the sense of becoming educated) from every event and every person that affects you until you become genuinely wise through openness to others—this is the humility required of any of us who wishes to comprehend the meaning of life. The real purpose of human language is not that we use words to talk but that we respond to one another so as to understand. This, you may remember from Chapter 2, is the ideal of service expressed in the tombs of Egyptian officials during the reign of King Izezi. This is also the humility, Ptahhatp tells us, that requires us to be quiet and listen.

'When your mind is overflowing, restrain your mouth.'

NOTES

1 Text after Perseus Digital Library
   Phaedrus 274ε–275β http://data.
   perseus.org/citations/urn:
   cts:greekLit:tlg0059.tlg012.
   perseus-grc1:274e.

INTRODUCTION

1 Section 774B, text after Bibliotheca
   Latina IntraText Digital Library
   Didascalicon http://www.intratext.
   com/IXT/LAT0506.
2 Gardiner (1917): 66.
3 Gunn (1912): 19.
4 Tobin (2003): 129. The assumption
   that the *Teaching of Ptahhatp* is no
   more than a practical and probably
   proscriptive statement of elitist
   attitudes remains widespread to
   this day, for which most recently see
   Diamond (2021).
5 Parkinson (1997): 247.
6 Lichtheim (1973): 62.
7 Readers with an Egyptological
   background may know that, a thousand
   years after the time of Ptahhatp, the
   vast royal cemetery of Egypt in the
   Valley of the Kings was presided over
   by a hill known as Meretseger, 'desiring
   silence'.
8 Hans Rösling's account of 'ten reasons
   why we're wrong about the world'
   is a fascinating analysis of how, as
   human beings, our chronic inability
   to recognize even simple facts is
   determined by all kinds of prejudicial
   thinking and essentially divorced
   from factors such as intelligence or
   education, see Rösling (2018).

9 Mansfield & Wildberger (2017): 395,
   concerning Columbia University tablet
   Plimpton 322.
10 Waddell (1940): 111 note 5.
11 For example, during the fourteenth
   century BC the name 'Amenhotep'
   was transcribed as Amanhatpe
   in the Akkadian texts of Amarna
   Letters 185 and 186 (Staatliche
   Museen in Berlin, tablets VAT1724
   and VAT1725), for which see Moran
   (1992): 265–8. Late Antique Coptic
   texts write this part of the verb (the
   stative) as *hatp* or *hotp*.
12 The name Ptahhatp (*pthḥtp* or *pthḥtpw*)
   is widely attested for many individuals
   in Old Kingdom and Middle Kingdom
   documents, see Ranke (1935): 141,
   which lists examples as 'numerous'
   ('mehrfach'). Consequently, the fact
   of it being a palindrome is no a priori
   basis for suspecting that the authorship
   is a fictitious ascription, for which
   argument see Breyer (2000/2001):
   21–2.
13 *The Histories*, Book II/77.
14 For example, see Dee et al. (2013).

CHAPTER 1

1 Catalogued according to the individual
   cut sheets as Département des
   Manuscrits, Égyptien 183–94.
2 See Dewachter (1985).
3 See Chabas (1858).
4 This is Žába (1956).
5 Ibid. 8–9.
6 Quirke (2004): 16.
7 Hrdlička (1928): 427.

8 Ibid. 426.

9 Ibid. 427.

10 Darwin (1871): 35.

11 Hume (1748/1993): 79.

12 See Manley (2014).

13 Spade (2007): 7–9.

14 Edwardes (2019): 5, which is a recent instance of how this paradigm is still embedded in a western scholarly account of human 'progress'.

15 Papyrus British Museum EA10057/10058.

16 Robins & Shute (1987): 58.

17 The possibility that there are lessons we can learn all over again from the ancients, even concerning applied subjects such as mathematics, is not at all facile. For example, regarding tablet Plimpton 322 (see page 13) Mansfield & Wildberger (2017): 415, note that 'within P322 there is a powerful alternative view of trigonometry based not on angles but on ratios of sides and squared quantities going back to Old Babylonian times. No subsequent table, from Hipparchus to Madhava to al-Kashi to Rheticus to the monumental 18th century French Cadastre, can compete with P322 with regards to precision—P322 is unique as it contains the world's only exact trigonometric table.'

18 Iversen (1993): 60.

19 Freedberg (2002): 400.

20 Godwin (2009): 12.

21 Ibid. 18.

22 Iversen (1993): 90.

23 Devlin (2009): 113.

24 Papyrus British Museum EA10684.

25 See Marciniak (1973); and Faulkner (1955): 27.

26 See Hagen (2009): 132–4.

27 Cairo JE 70105, see Ryholt (2021): 24.

28 See Gunn (1928); and Dreyer (1987).

29 See Tallet (2017); and Tallet & Lehner (2022).

30 See P. Posener-Kriéger (1994); and P. Posener-Kriéger (2004).

31 Regulski (2016): 9.

32 Parker (2008): 19.

33 See Moran (1992).

34 For a fascinating argument in favour of this conclusion, see Part One of Wiseman (1977).

35 Five hundred or more letters and documents written in the Ancient Egyptian language but on clay tablets rather than ostraca constitute a singular discovery made at Dakhla, more than 300 kilometres (200 miles) west of the Nile Valley, see Pantalacci (2013). They certainly derive from the Old Kingdom administration and doubtless represent the practical adaptation of the Egyptian writing tradition to a specific location in a distant, desert oasis.

36 The latest dated documents written on papyrus in Coptic and in Arabic are dated to the years 942 and 981 respectively, see Buzi & Emmell (2015): 137.

37 Parkinson & Quirke (1995): 65.

38 Ibid. 16.

39 Though page six has only eleven lines.

40 Jéquier (1911): 8.

41 Černý (1952): 30; see also Ryholt (2021).

42 Gamble (1995): 47.

43 The Great Harris Papyrus = Papyrus British Museum EA 9999.

44 See also Hagen (2012).

45 Dévaud (1916).

46 Gardiner (1917): 65.

47 Žába (1956): 10 ('ne supposant qu'un nombre très restreint d'erreurs dans le texte, je ne l'émende que deux ou trois fois').

48 See Caminos (1956): 52–4 with plates 28–30.

49 Panov (2021) is now an updated synoptic edition of the text.

50 Chabas (1858): 3 ('l'ecriture a été soigneusement effacée et le papyrus lustré de nouveau').

51 Papyrus Hermitage 1115.

52 See Bomhard (1999).

53 Papyrus British Museum EA 10371 + 10435.

54 Jéquier (1911): 10. In fact, the book reached the British Museum in such poor condition that the various fragments have been registered as two separate series.

55 Roccati (2014): 239; see also Heyne (2006).

56 Stephen Quirke found that a detailed study of papyrus fragments 'highlighted for me the material presence of the literary book as a distinctive object category, in formal features such as the handwriting style, spacing of signs and lines, and sometimes the combination of vertical and horizontal lines for segments of writing', Quirke (2004): 27.

57 Cairo JE 41790.

58 A smaller writing board (Carnarvon Tablet 2) found among the same debris has the fragmentary text of a Teaching and may possibly be a fragment of the same copy, see Gardiner (1916): 95–6.

59 Papyrus British Museum EA 10509.

60 Announcement, *The New York Times*, 21 October 1907: 7. Murch collected other significant artefacts, see for example Moran (1992): xiv.

61 Quirke (2004): 17 (Group Four).

62 See Černý (1952): 24–5.

63 Papyrus Turin CGT 54014.

64 The top of the page is damaged and the beginning of each line lost, so originally there might have been other lines above the extant writing. Nevertheless, by comparison with the other copies the only text missing from the beginning is the phrase which itself means 'beginning' (ḥat-'a).

65 Ostraca IFAO o.DeM.1232, 1233 and 1234, for which see Posener (1972).

66 Papyrus Turin 1874.

67 Quote taken from the title page of Sotheby's catalogue for the auction of the collection.

68 Quirke (2004): 15–16 (Group One). They are Papyrus British Museum EA10274 and Papyrus Berlin 3022–5, together with various fragments eventually purchased in 1912 and now in the Pierpont Morgan Library in New York.

69 Papyrus Berlin 3033, for which see Blackman (1988). This book was originally edited and published as Erman (1890).

70 The text in Papyrus Westcar has often been dated specifically to the late Middle Kingdom on the basis of internal grammatical criteria, such as the alleged use of a definite article. In fact, the criteria in question are too few and too ambiguous to support a definitive argument, so such chronological precision is entirely spurious. The book's date of composition effectively remains any time, however recent or distant, before Papyrus Westcar itself was copied out.

71 Presented to the New York Academy of Medicine in 1948.

72 Displayed in the Schauraum Papyrus Ebers of the Bibliotheca Albertina.

73 Quirke (2004): 16–17 (Group Three).

74 Usually referred to together as P.Boulaq 18.

75 See Mariette (1872): 6–8 (number 18).

76 Quirke (1990): 12–13.

77 Quirke (2004): 16 (Group Two); see also Quibell (1898): 3–4. The tomb's present location is uncertain, for which see Downing & Parkinson (2016).

78 Papyrus British Museum EA10326/ recto 14–verso 1.

79 Quirke (2004): 12.

80 Another putative literary text, the so-called *Loyalist Teaching*, is not known from any book at this early date but part of the text appears in the hieroglyphic inscription on a funerary monument from the late Twelfth Dynasty (Cairo CG 20538).

81 See Pérez-Accino (2015).

82 Lichtheim (1973): 6.

83 Quirke (2004): 90.

84 Lichtheim (1973): 7.

85 Ibid. 62, where Lichtheim also takes into consideration what she understands to be the moral, intellectual and literary evolution of Egyptians during the Old Kingdom.

86 For example, these include the negation -*w* and a reduplicating future passive form. The relevance of these is that they are *ordinarily* treated in Egyptology as definitive aspects of Old Egyptian grammar and in Middle Egyptian as rare archaisms.

87 Quirke (2004): 36.

88 Jéquier (1911): 11 ('sans attacher une importance exagérée à l'exactitude phraséologique du texte').

89 Roccati (2014): 239–40.

CHAPTER 2

1 John Duns Scotus (1891): *Quaestiones subtilissimæ super libros metaphysicorum Aristotelis*. Opera Omnia, 7. Vivès, Paris: 4.

2 Morenz (2020): 607.

3 See Butzer (1960).

4 For a recent attempt to explain Old Kingdom Egypt by applying evolutionary theory to funerary architecture and archaeology, see Bárta (2015).

5 Saqqara tomb LS 6, now Berlin ÄM 1105.

6 *Denkmäler aus Aegypten und Aethiopien*, Textband I: 143 ('scharf, gut und fein poliert', 'schwerfällig und etwas stillos').

7 Berlin ÄM 1106.

8 For a helpful summary of the broader social consequences of pyramid-building, quite apart from other industrial activities, see Tallet & Lehner (2022): Chapter 15.

9 See Bell (1970): 572.

10 Palermo Stone: recto III/4.

11 Giza tomb LG 87.

12 Cairo JE 1432.

13 See also Hagen with Soliman (2018).

14 Megahed et al. (2017): 48.

15 Megahed et al. (2019): 32–3.

16 The decorated tomb of Pepyankh-Setju and other anonymous tombs immediately beside Izezi's pyramid seem to be later intrusions, and nothing would seem to connect these people with Izezi's family, see Megahed et al. (2017): 42–8.

17 See Dodson & Hilton (2004): 67.

18 Saqqara tomb 85 (D 8).

19 Saqqara tomb 80 (D 3).

20 Saqqara tomb 84 (D 7).

21 Saqqara tomb 82 (D 5).

22 Brooklyn 64.148.2.

23 Saqqara tomb D 62.

24 Nuzzolo with Zanfagna (2017): 271.

25 Potentially there is also a sixth vizier, named Ptahhatpdesher or 'Red' Ptahhatp but his specific dating is not known, see Maspero (1885): mastaba F. 4.

26 Saqqara tomb D 64.

27 Following, for example, the practice of *Lexikon der Ägyptologie*, see Martin-Pardey (1982): 1181.

28 Saqqara tombs C 6 and C 7.

29 Saqqara tomb LS 31.

30 As well as Ptahhatp's son Akhethatp, there are Seshemnefer (III) (Giza G 5170), Rashepses (Saqqara LS 16), Snedjemib-Inti (Giza G 2370 and LG 10) and Tjenti (Saqqara C 18).

31 Snedjemib-Inti's wife has the name Tjefi, which is a feminine form of Ptahhatp's family cognomen, Tjefu.

32 The presumed order in which they held office could be modified to take account of Kanawati's suggestion that the principle of two viziers serving in office at one time might have been instituted during the reign of Izezi, see Kanawati (1980): 11. However, this possibility must be set against the prevailing tendency of modern scholarship to treat the reign of Izezi as no longer than twenty-eight years. Moreover, if this reform actually happened at this time, it would seem to be linked to the institution of the office of 'Overseer of the Nile Valley', which also came about during the reign of Izezi and the first holder of this new office was Akhethatp—the son of Ptahhatp (I) and his eventual successor as vizier, see Clarke (2009): 123–4. In other words, Kanawati's suggestion does not significantly increase the likelihood that there were several more viziers named Ptahhatp during Izezi's reign.

33 The attribution of specific viziers to the reigns of particular kings earlier than Izezi in the Fifth Dynasty is especially uncertain.

34 Maspero (1885): 123–4.

35 See the discussion in Nuzzolo with Zanfagna (2017): 271–74.

36 See Quirke (1990).

37 Maspero (1885): 351 ('surtout par la perfection des sculptures qui décorent la chambre principale').

38 Saqqara tomb D 64.

39 Saqqara tomb E 14.

40 Cairo Museum JE 1732.

41 Cairo JE 72379/80.

42 Cairo JE 72204/5/6 and JE 72209 (cylinder seal). However, Fischer read the royal name on the cylinder seal not as Djedkara (Izezi) but as Nefrefra, who was king earlier in the Fifth Dynasty, see Fischer (1972): 14.

43 MFA 27.442 from Giza tomb G 7510.

44 See Tallet & Lehner (2022): Chapter 12.

45 Giza tomb G 7510.

46 Roemer und Pelizaeus Museum 1962 from Giza tomb G 4000.

47 Louvre E 3023.

48 Saqqara tomb D 10.

49 Cairo JE 1482 (right side).

50 See Allon & Navrátilová (2017): 23 & 147–8.

51 Text at Lepsius *Denkmäler aus Aegypten und Aethiopien*, Abtheilung II: plate 76 c–f; see also Taterka (2017).

52 Giza tomb G 53.

53 Papyrus Berlin P.8869, for which see Smither (1942).

54 See Verner (2010).

55 Louvre E 5323, which is 16 cm (6¼ in.) tall.

56 See Goedicke (1956).

57 See Wilkinson (2000): 90–91.

58 For these early examples see Jiménez-Serrano (2002).

59 Palermo Stone, recto VI/2–4.

60 See also Nuzzolo (2015).

61 Pyramid Texts speech 407: 3–5, text after Allen (2013).

62 Pyramid Texts speech 412: 16, text after Allen (2013).

CHAPTER 3

1 Text after Gardiner (1946): plate XIV.
2 Is there perhaps some lost or mistaken connection between the names Kairsu and Kagemni, see Barta (1980)?
3 Saqqara tomb LS 10.
4 Gardiner (1946): 71.
5 Ibid. 74.
6 Brooklyn 37.1394E, which measures 140 × 95 × 15 cm (55 × 37 × 6 in.).
7 See Helck (1984).
8 See Brunner-Traut (1940): 7.
9 Lichtheim (1973): 6.
10 Papyrus British Museum EA10508.

CHAPTER 4

1 Gunn (1912): 14–15.
2 Ibid. 12–13.
3 For the definitive account of the various motivations behind the decipherment process, see Iversen (1993).
4 Quoted by Ray (1991): 52.
5 Lewis (2002b): 24.
6 Jéquier (1911): 6 ('le texte littéraire égyptien le plus difficile à traduire'). The same comment is made by Peet (1931): 101.
7 Gardiner JEA 4 (1917): 66.
8 Peet (1931): 100 note 1.
9 Gardiner (1946): 72–73.
10 De Buck (1932).
11 From a letter of 1852, quoted by Campbell & Garnett (1882): 180.
12 A summary of the topic may be found in Parkinson (1995).
13 For example, Parkinson (1997): 270; and Tobin (2003): 143.
14 Parkinson (1997): 248.
15 *Cymbeline* Act 2, scene 5.
16 From the Preface to Boethius, *The Consolation of Philosophy* (Folio Society, London, 1998).
17 Kierkegaard (1849): 1.C.A.(a).β

('Ethvert Menneske er nemlig primitivt anlagt som et Selv, bestemt til at blive sig selv').
18 Passage 303, text after Chaîne (1960): 30 ('ϩⲙ ⲡⲓⲣⲁⲥⲙⲟⲥ ⲛⲓⲙ ⲙⲡⲣⲟⲛⲁⲣⲓⲕⲉ ⲉⲣⲱⲙⲉ ⲁⲗⲗⲁ ⲟⲛⲁⲣⲓⲕⲉ ⲉⲣⲟⲕ ⲙⲁⲩⲁⲁⲕ ⲉⲕⲭⲱ ⲙⲙⲟⲥ ⲭⲉ ⲉⲣⲉ ⲛⲁⲓ ϣⲟⲟⲡ ⲙⲙⲟⲓ ⲉⲧⲃⲉ ⲛⲁⲛⲟⲃⲉ').
19 See Quirke (2004): 12; also Manley (2020).
20 For the significance of this, see Manley (2017): 92–94, 259; also Manley (2014).
21 P. Leiden 371/recto 1–4.
22 Morton (1995): 570.

CHAPTER 5

1 Faith & Culture with Joseph Pearce. 126, *Paganism with Fr. Longenecker*. Augustine Institute. Originally broadcast 1 June 2020, beginning @ 4 mins 15 secs.
2 Faith & Culture with Joseph Pearce. 102, *Myth and the Bible with Fr. Longenecker*. Augustine Institute. Originally broadcast 13 April 2020, beginning @ 8 mins.
3 The Crossway Podcast. 112, *Delighting in the Ten Commandments*. Originally broadcast 29 March 2021, beginning @ 28 mins 41 secs.
4 Warburton (2009): 85.
5 Nyord (2018): 74.
6 Popielska-Grzybowska (2009).
7 BBC Recording T7324W. *A Debate on the Existence of God. The Cosmological Argument*, with F. C. Copleston and B. A. W. Russell. Originally broadcast 28 January 1948.
8 Popielska-Grzybowska (2011): 680.
9 Lewis (2002a): 18.
10 'Des Menschen Maß ist's. Voll Verdienst, doch dichterisch, wohnet Der Mensch auf dieser Erde' — a verse taken from Friedrich Hölderlin's poem *In lieblicher*

Bläue (1808) which was interpreted in terms of the concept of 'being' by the German philosopher Martin Heidegger in a famous 1951 lecture.

11 Manley (2014): 205.

12 British Museum EA498.

13 Bodine (2009): 6.

14 El Hawary (2010): 79 ('die Zeichen wurden zwar elegant, aber schwach eingraviert').

15 Ibid. 74–9.

16 https://www.britishmuseum.org/collection/object/Y_EA498 accessed 24 December, 2021.

17 Initially, see Junge (1973).

18 Krauss (1999).

19 A helpful summary of various arguments about the dating may be found in El Hawary (2010): 92–111.

20 Altenmüller (1975): col. 1068 ('die Datierung des Denkmals ist umstritten').

21 Morkot & James (2009): 21.

22 See Maystre (1992): 4–13.

23 Ibid. 193–214. The family is well attested through a group of stelae from tombs at Memphis, specifically EA147, EA184, EA188 and EA886 in the British Museum, and UC14357 in the Petrie Museum of Egyptian Archaeology, London.

24 The seminal criticism of this modern narrative may be found in Morkot (2000).

25 Taylor (2000): 348.

26 Nineveh tablet RINAP4 1019 (= British Museum K8692): obverse 21–23, text after http://oracc.museum.upenn.edu/rinap/rinap4/corpus ('*ana ēkallātišu mašši'ti ... aššātišu mārīšu u mārātišu [ša] kīma šâšuma kīma kupri ṣalmu šīrūšunu*').

27 Therefore 'to use them as dividing lines in works on history, art, administration,

or any other continuous aspect of ancient Egyptian civilization may be arbitrary and historically unwarranted', Malek (1982): 106.

28 Taylor (2000): 341.

29 Aston (2020): 685.

30 Ibid. 686–7 is a recent discussion of the putative impact of 'Egyptian', 'Libyan' and 'Kushite' identities on pharaonic burial practices.

31 Ibid. 689.

32 Morkot (2000): 134.

33 For example, compare the arguments of Kahn (2001) and Broekman (2015).

34 Cairo JE 48863, lines 3–6.

35 Morkot & James (2009): 26–30.

36 The archaeological development of the cemetery is often still interpreted on the simple basis that tombs which are smaller and 'strongly Nubian in character' are earlier, while tombs 'characterized by more Egyptian-inspired features' are later, Taylor (2000): 346. On the other hand, some scholars have argued that the earliest tombs here may well date from the period of Egyptian New Kingdom control of Nubia, see Morkot (2000): 138–44.

37 2 Chronicles 12.

38 See the summary discussion with references in Aston (2020): 694–703.

39 For example, compare the reconstructions of Aston (2020), Kitchen (2009) and Dodson & Hilton (2004): 217.

40 El Hawary (2010): 92.

41 See Manley (2013).

42 See Morkot (2007).

43 Aston (2020): 687.

44 Cairo JE 44665.

45 See Török (1997): 161–70.

46 For at least a century, since Breasted (1901), the columns have

conventionally been numbered as though the heading for the account of creation were separate from the columns below it, so the conventional numbering used here gives (lines) 1–2, then (columns) 3–64.

47 Lewis (2012): 246.

48 Hawking (1988): 139.

49 Ibid. 46.

50 Wittgenstein (1922): statement I ('Die Welt is alles, was der Fall ist').

51 For a compelling description of reality by a modern physicist in terms of a timeless 'now' rather than 'the arrow of time', see Barbour (1999).

52 See *Phaedrus*, sections 244–5, a short dialogue which , interestingly enough, precedes Socrates' own account of the Non-being of the creator, which may be compared to the discussion of the Shabaka Stone below. See also Pieper (1995).

53 Jung (1976): paragraph 601.

54 For a helpful discussion of the relationship between meaning and information in this context, see Lennox (2009): 148–62.

55 *The Book of Common Prayer*. 1853 'Pickering' Edition. William Allan, London: 420 (§22).

BIBLIOGRAPHY

Allen, J.P. (2013). *A New Concordance of the Pyramid Texts*. Brown University, Providence.

Allon, N. & H. Navrátilová (2017). *Ancient Egyptian Scribes: A cultural exploration*. Bloomsbury, London & New York.

Altenmüller, H. (1975). 'Denkmal memphitischer Theologie.' In W. Helck, E. Otto & E. Feucht-Putz (eds). *Lexikon der Ägyptologie* I. Otto Harrassowitz, Wiesbaden: 1065–69.

Aston, D. (2020). 'The Third Intermediate Period.' In Shaw & Bloxam (2020): 684–719.

Barbour, J. (1999). *The End of Time*. Weidenfeld & Nicolson, London.

Bárta, M. (2015). 'Ancient Egyptian History as an Example of Punctuated Equilibrium: An outline.' In Der Manuelian & Schneider (2015): 1–17.

Bárta, M., F. Coppens & J. Krejčí (eds). (2011). *Abusir and Saqqara in the Year 2010*. Charles University, Prague.

— (2017). *Abusir and Saqqara in the Year 2015*. Charles University, Prague.

Barta, W. (1980). 'Lehre für Kagemni.' In W. Helck, W. Westendorf & R. Drenkhahn (eds). *Lexikon der Ägyptologie* III. Otto Harrassowitz, Wiesbaden: 980–82.

Bell, B. (1970). 'The Oldest Records of the Nile Floods.' *The Geographical Journal* 136/4: 569–73.

Blackman, A.M. (1988). *The Story of King Kheops and the Magicians*. J. V. Books, Reading.

Bodine, J.J. (2009). 'The Shabaka Stone: An introduction.' *Studia Antiqua* 7/1: article 3.

Bomhard, A-S. von (1999). 'Le conte du naufragé et le Papyrus Prisse.' *Revue d'Égyptologie* 50: 51–56.

Breasted, J.H. (1901). 'The Philosophy of a Memphite Priest.' *Zeitschrift für ägyptische Sprache und Altertumskunde* 39: 40–54.

Breyer, F.A.K. (2000/2001). 'Ptahhotep—von Ptahs Gnaden der Weise mit dem dreifachen Palindrom.' *Die Welt des Orients* 31: 19–22.

Broekman, G.P.F. (2015). 'The Order of Succession Between Shabaka and Shabataka: A different view on the chronology of the Twenty-fifth Dynasty.' *Göttinger Miszellen* 245: 17–31.

Brunner-Traut, E. (1940). 'Die Weisheitslehre des Djedef-Hor.' *Zeitschrift für ägyptische Sprache und Altertumskunde* 76: 3–9.

Butzer, K.W. (1960). 'Environment and Human Ecology in Egypt during Predynastic and Early Dynastic Times.' *Bulletin de la Société de Géographie d'Egypte* 32: 43–47.

Buzi, P. & S. Emmell (2015). 'Coptic Codicology.' In A. Bausi, P.G. Borbone, F. Briquel-Chatonnet, P. Buzi, J. Gippert, C. Macé, M. Maniaci, Z. Melissakis,

L.E. Parodi & W. Witakowski. *Comparative Oriental Manuscript Studies: An introduction*. Tredition, Hamburg: 137–53.

Caminos, R.A. (1956). *Literary Fragments in the Hieratic Script*. Griffith Institute, Oxford.

Campbell, L. & W. Garnett (1882). *The Life of James Clerk Maxwell with a selection from his correspondence and occasional writings and a sketch of his contributions to Science*. Macmillan & Co, London.

Černý, J. (1952). *Paper and Books in Ancient Egypt*. H. K. Lewis & Co, London.

Chabas, F. (1858). 'Le plus ancient livre du monde. Étude sur le Papyrus Prisse.' *Revue Archéologique* April–September 1858: 1–25.

Chaîne, M. (1960). *Le manuscrit de la version Copte en dialecte Sahidique des 'Apophthegmata patrum'*. Institut Français d'archéologie Orientale, Cairo.

Clarke, T. (2009). Thesis. *The Overseer of Upper Egypt in Egypt's Old Kingdom. 1, Text*. Macquarie University, Melbourne.

Darwin, C.R. (1871). *The Descent of Man and Selection in Relation To Sex*. 2nd edn. John Murray, London.

De Buck, A. (1932). 'Het religieus Karakter der oudste egyptische Wijsheid.' *Nieuw Theologisch Tijdschrift* 21: 322–49.

Dee, M., D. Wengrow, A. Shortland, A. Stevenson, F. Brock, L. Girdland Flink & C. Bronk Ramsey (2013). 'An Absolute Chronology for Early Egypt Using Radiocarbon Dating and Bayesian Statistical Modelling.' *Proceedings of the Royal Society* 469 (doi.org/10.1098/rspa.2013.0395).

Der Manuelian, P. & T. Schneider (eds). (2015). *Towards a New History for the Egyptian Old Kingdom: Perspectives on the Pyramid Age*. Brill, Leiden & Boston.

Dévaud, E. (1916). *Les maximes de Ptahhotep d'aprés le papyrus Prisse, les papyrus 10371/10435 et 10509 du British Museum et la tablette Carnarvon. Texte.* Lithographie P. Bättig, Fribourg.

Devlin, F.R. (2009). 'The Revolution in Human Evolution (review article).' *The Occidental Quarterly* 9/2: 113–27.

Dewachter, M. (1985). 'Nouvelles informations relatives à l'exploitation de la nécropole royale de Drah Aboul Neggah'. *Révue d'Égyptologie* 36: 43–66.

Diamond, K-A. (2021). 'Masculinities and the Mechanisms of Hegemony in the Instruction of Ptahhotep.' In C. Geisen, J. Li, S. Shubert & K. Yamamoto (eds). *His Good Name: Essays on Identity and Self-presentation in Ancient Egypt in Honor of Ronald J. Leprohon*. Lockwood Press, Atlanta: 29–46.

Dodson, A.M. & D. Hilton (2004). *The Complete Royal Families of Ancient Egypt*. Thames & Hudson, London & New York.

Downing, M. & R.B. Parkinson (2016). 'The Tomb of the Ramesseum Papyri in the Newberry Papers, The Griffith Institute Oxford.' *British Museum Studies in Ancient Egypt and Sudan* 23: 35–45.

Dreyer, G. (1987). 'Drei archaisch-hieratische Gefässaufschriften mit Jahresnamen aus Elephantine.' In J. Osing & G. Dreyer. *Form und Mass: Beiträge zur Literatur, Sprache und Kunst des alten Ägypten*. Ägypten und Altes Testament 12. Otto Harrassowitz, Wiesbaden: 98–109.

Edwardes, M.P.J. (2019). *Origins of the Self: An anthropological perspective.*
UCL Press, London.

Erman, A. (1890). *Die Märchen des Papyrus Westcar.* Mittheilungen aus den
orientalischen Sammlungen V–VI. W. Spemann, Berlin.

Faulkner, R.O. (1955). 'The Installation of the Vizier.' *Journal of Egyptian
Archaeology* 41: 18–29.

Fischer, H.G. (1972). 'Old Kingdom Cylinder Seals for the Lower Classes.'
Metropolitan Museum Journal 6: 5–16.

Freedberg, D. (2002). *The Eye of the Lynx: Galileo, his friends, and the beginnings
of modern natural history.* University of Chicago Press, Chicago.

Gamble, H.Y. (1995). *Books and Readers in the Early Christian Church: A history
of early Christian texts.* Yale University Press, New Haven & London.

Gardiner, A.H. (1916). 'The Defeat of the Hyksos by Kamōse. The Carnarvon
Tablet, No. I.' *Journal of Egyptian Archaeology* 3: 95–110.

— (1917). Review of Dévaud (1916). *Journal of Egyptian Archaeology* 4: 65–6.

— (1946). 'The Instruction Addressed to Kagemni and His Brethren.' *Journal of
Egyptian Archaeology* 32: 71–74.

— (1951). 'Kagemni Once Again.' *Journal of Egyptian Archaeology* 37: 109–10.

Godwin, J. (2009). *Athanasius Kircher's Theatre of the World.* Thames & Hudson,
London & New York.

Goedicke, H. (1956). 'The Pharaoh *ny-swtḥ.*' *Zeitschrift für ägyptische Sprache und
Altertumskunde* 81: 18–24.

Gunn, B. (1912). *The Instruction of Ptah-Hotep and the Instruction of Ke'gemni:
The Oldest Books in the World.* John Murray, London.

— (1928). 'Inscriptions from the Step Pyramid Site. III, fragments of inscribed
vessels.' *Annales du Service des Antiquitiés de l'Égypte* 28: 153–74.

Hagen, F. (2009). 'Echoes of "Ptahhotep" in the Greco-Roman Period?' *Zeitschrift
für ägyptische Sprache und Altertumskunde* 136: 130–35.

— (2012). *An Ancient Egyptian Literary Text in Context: The Instruction of
Ptahhotep.* Orientalia Lovaniensia Analecta 218. Peeters, Leuven.

Hagen, F. & D. Soliman (2018). 'Archives in Ancient Egypt, 2500–1000 BCE.'
In A. Bausi, C. Brockman, M. Friedrich & S. Kienitz (eds). *Manuscripts and
Archives.* Studies in Manuscript Cultures 11. De Gruyter, Berlin: 71–90.

El Hawary, A. (2010). *Wortschöpfung. Die Memphitische Theologie und die Siegesstele
des Pije – zwei Zeugen kultureller Repräsentation in der 25. Dynastie.* Orbis
Biblicus et Orientalis 243. Fribourg & Göttingen.

Hawking, S. (1988). *A Brief History of Time: From the Big Bang to black holes.*
Bantam Press, New York.

Helck, W. (1984). *Die Lehre des Djedefhor und die Lehre eines Vaters an seinen Sohn.*
Otto Harrassowitz, Wiesbaden.

Heyne, A. (2006). 'The Teaching of Ptahhotep: the London versions.' In M.
Cannata (ed.). *Current Research in Egyptology 2006. Proceedings of the seventh
annual symposium.* Oxbow, Oxford: 85–98.

Hrdlička, A. (1928). 'The Evidence Bearing on Man's Evolution.' *The Smithsonian Report for 1927*. Smithsonian Institution Press, Washington, D.C.

Hume, D. (1748/1993). *An Enquiry Concerning Human Understanding with a 'Letter' and 'Abstract of a Treatise'*. 2nd edn. Hackett Publishing, Indiana.

Iversen, E. (1993). *The Myth of Egypt and Its Hieroglyphs in European Tradition*. Princeton University Press, Princeton.

Jéquier, G. (1911). *Le papyrus Prisse et ses variantes*. Librairie Paul Geuthner, Paris.

Jiménez-Serrano, A. (2002). *Royal Festivals in the Late Predynastic Period and the First Dynasty*. BAR International Series 1076. Archaeopress, Oxford.

Jung, C. (1976). *The Symbolic Life: Miscellaneous writings*. The Collected Works 18. Princeton University Press, Princeton.

Junge, F. (1973). 'Zur Fehldatierung des sog. Denkmals memphitischer Theologie oder der Beitrag der ägyptischen Theologie zur Geistesgeschichte der Spätzeit.' *Mitteilungen des Deutschen Archäologischen Instituts Abteilung Kairo* 29: 195–204.

Kahn, D. (2001). 'The Inscription of Sargon II at Tang-i Var and the Chronology of Dynasty 25.' *Orientalia* 70: 1–18.

Kanawati, N. (1980). *Governmental Reforms in Old Kingdom Egypt*. Aris & Phillips, Warminster.

Kierkegaard, S. (1849). *Sygdommen til Døden (Sickness Unto Death)*. Det Kgl. Biblioteks tekstportal (https://tekster.kb.dk), Copenhagen.

Kitchen, K.A. (2009). 'The Third Intermediate Period in Egypt: An overview of fact and fiction.' In G.P.F. Broekman, R.J. Demarée & O.E. Kaper (eds). *The Libyan Period in Egypt: Historical and Cultural Studies into the 21st–24th Dynasties*. Leiden Egyptologische Uitgaven 23. Nederlands Instituut voor het Nabije Oosten & Peeters, Leuven: 161–202.

Krauss, R. (1999). 'Wie jung ist die memphitische Philosophie auf dem Schabako-Stein?' In E. Teeter & J.A. Larson (eds). *Gold of praise. Studies on ancient Egypt in honor of E.F. Wente*. Studies in Ancient Oriental Civilization 58. The Oriental Institute, Chicago: 239–46.

Lennox, J.C. (2009). *God's Undertaker: Has Science Buried God?* Lion Hudson, Oxford.

Lewis, C.S. (2002a). 'Is Theology Poetry?' In L. Walmsley (ed.). *C. S. Lewis Essay Collection: Faith, Christianity and the Church*. HarperCollins, Hammersmith: 10–21.

— (2002b). 'The Funeral of a Great Myth.' Ibid. 22–32.

— (2012). *Miracles*. Signature Classics Edition. Collins, London.

Lichtheim, M. (1973). *Ancient Egyptian Literature. 1, The Old and Middle Kingdoms*. University of California Press, Berkeley.

Málek, J. (1982). 'The original version of the Royal Canon of Turin.' *Journal of Egyptian Archaeology* 68: 93–106.

Manley, W.P. (2013). 'Anaximander.' In R. Bagnall, K. Brodersen, C. Champion, A. Erskine & S. Huebner (eds). *The Encyclopedia of Ancient History*. Wiley-Blackwell, Oxford: 409–10.

— (2014). 'A Very Bright Poet, a Long Time Ago. Considerations of Language, Meaning and the Mind during the Bronze Age.' In A.M. Dodson, J.J. Johnston & W. Monkhouse (eds). *A Good Scribe and an Exceedingly Wise Man: Studies in honour of W.J. Tait*. Golden House Publications, London: 199–212.

— (2017). *Egyptian Art*. Thames & Hudson, London & New York.

— (2020). 'Literary Texts.' In Shaw & Bloxam (2020): 1005–16.

Mansfield, D.F. & N.J. Wildberger (2017). 'Plimpton 322 is Babylonian exact sexagesimal trigonometry.' *Historia Mathematica* 44: 395–419.

Marciniak, M. (1973). 'Une formule empruntée à la sagesse de Ptahhotep.' *Bulletin de l'Institut Français d'archéologie Orientale* 73: 109–12.

Mariette, A. (1872). *Les papyrus égyptiens du Musée de Boulaq. II, papyrus no. 10–20*. Librairie A. Franck, F. Vieweg, Paris.

Martin-Pardey, E. (1982). 'Ptahhotep.' In W. Helck, W. Westendorf & R. Drenkhahn (eds). *Lexikon der Ägyptologie* IV. Otto Harrassowitz, Wiesbaden: 1181.

Maspero, G. (1885). *Les mastabas de l'Ancien Empire: Fragment du dernier ouvrage de A. Mariette*. F. Vieweg, Paris.

Maystre, C. (1992). *Les grands prêtres de Ptah de Memphis*. Orbis Biblicus et Orientalis 113. Universitätsverlag Freiburg Schweiz, Vandenhoeck & Ruprecht, Göttingen.

Megahed, M., P. Jánosi & H. Vymazalová (2017). 'Djedkare's pyramid complex: Preliminary Report of the 2016 season.' *Prague Egyptological Studies* 19: 37–52.

— (2019). 'Exploration of the pyramid complex of King Djedkare: Season 2018.' *Prague Egyptological Studies* 23: 12–36.

Moran, W.L. (1992). *The Amarna Letters*. Johns Hopkins University Press, Baltimore & London.

Morenz, L. (2020). 'The Early Dynastic Period.' In Shaw & Bloxam (2020): 596–618.

Morkot, R.G. (2000). *The Black Pharaohs*. Rubicon, London.

— (2007). 'Tradition, Innovation, and Researching the Past in Libyan, Kushite, and Saïte Egypt.' In H. Crawford (ed.). *Regime Change in the Ancient Near East and Egypt from Sargon of Agade to Saddam Hussein*. Proceedings of the British Academy 136. The British Academy, London: 141–64.

Morkot, R.G. & P. James (2009). 'Peftjauawybast, King of Nen-nesut: Genealogy, Art History, and the Chronology of late Libyan Egypt.' *Antiguo Oriente* 7: 13–55.

Morton, A. (1995). 'Mind.' In T. Honderich (ed.). *The Oxford Companion to Philosophy*. Oxford University Press, Oxford: 569–70.

Nuzzolo, M. (2015). 'The Sed-Festival of Niuserra and the Fifth Dynasty Sun-Temples.' In Der Manuelian & Schneider (2015): 366–92.

Nuzzolo, M. & P. Zanfagna (2017). 'Patterns of Tomb Placement in the Memphite Necropolis: Fifth-dynasty Saqqara in context.' In Bárta et al. (2017): 257–92.

Nyord, R. (2018). '"Taking Ancient Egyptian Mortuary Religion Seriously": Why would we, and how could we?' *Journal of Ancient Egyptian Interconnections* 17: 73–87.

Panov, M. (2021). *The Manuscripts of the Maxims of Ptahhotep*. Egyptian Texts XVII. Panov, Novosibersk.

Pantalacci, L. (2013). 'Balat, a Frontier Town and its Archive.' In J.C. Moreno García (ed.). *Ancient Egyptian Administration*. Handbook of Oriental Studies 104. Brill, Leiden: 197–214.

Parker, D.C. (2008). *An Introduction to the New Testament Manuscripts and their Texts*. Cambridge University Press, Cambridge.

Parkinson, R.B. (1995). '"Homosexual" Desire and Middle Kingdom Literature.' *Journal of Egyptian Archaeology* 81: 57–76.

— (1997). *The Tale of Sinuhe and Other Ancient Egyptian Poems 1940–1640 BC*. Oxford World's Classics, Oxford.

— (2002). *Poetry and Culture in Middle Kingdom Egypt: A dark side to perfection*. Equinox Publishing, London.

— (2009). *Reading Ancient Egyptian Poetry Among Other Histories*. Wiley-Blackwell, Oxford.

Parkinson, R.B. & S.J. Quirke (1995). *Papyrus*. British Museum Press, London.

Peet, T.E. (1931). *A Comparative Study of the Literatures of Egypt, Palestine and Mesopotamia*. The British Academy, London.

Pérez-Accino, J-R. (2015). 'Who is the Sage Talking About? Neferty and the Egyptian sense of history.' In P. Kousoulis & N. Lazaridis (eds). *Proceedings of the Tenth International Congress of Egyptologists, University of the Aegean, Rhodes, 22–29 May 2008*, 2. Peeters, Leuven: 1495–1502.

Pieper, J. (1995). *Divine Madness: Plato's case against secular humanism*. Ignatius Press, San Francisco.

Popielska-Grzybowska, J. (2009). 'Figuratively Speaking … — The Question of the Use of Figurative Language in the Pyramid Texts.' In J. Popielska-Grzybowska, O. Białostocka & J. Iwaszczuk (eds). *Proceedings of the Third Central European Conference of Young Egyptologists. Egypt 2004. Perspectives of Research*. Acta Archaeologica Pultuskiensia 1, Pułtusk: 157–63.

— (2011). 'Religious Reality Creation through Language in the Old Kingdom Religious Texts.' In Bárta et al.: 680–93.

Posener, G. (1972). *Catalogue des ostraca hiératiques littéraires de Deir el-Medineh*. IFAO, Cairo.

Posener-Kriéger, P. (1994). 'Le coffret de Gebelein.' In C. Berger, G. Clerc & N. Grimal (eds). *Hommages à Jean Leclant* I. Bibliothèque d'Étude 106/1. Institut Français d'archéologie Orientale, Cairo: 315–26.

— (2004). *I Papiri di Gebelein (scavi G. Farina 1935)*. Studi del Museo Egizio di Torino Gebelein 1, Turin.

Quack, J.F. (2005). 'Ein neuer Zugang zur Lehre des Ptahhotep.' *Die Welt des Orients* 35: 7–21.

Quibell, J.E. (1898). *The Ramesseum*. Egyptian Research Account, London.

Quirke, S.J. (1990). *The Administration of Egypt in the Late Middle Kingdom: The hieratic documents*. SIA Publishing, London.

— (1992). *Ancient Egyptian Religion*. British Museum Press, London.

— (2004). *Egyptian Literature 1800 BC. Questions and Readings*. Golden House Publications, London.

Ranke, H. (1935). *Die ägyptischen Personennamen. I, Verzeichnis der Namen*. J. J. Augustin, Glückstadt.

Ray, J. (1991). 'The Name of the First: Thomas Young and the Decipherment of Egyptian Writing.' *Journal of the Ancient Chronology Forum* 4: 49–54.

Regulski, I. (2016). 'The Origins and Early Development of Writing in Egypt.' *Oxford Handbooks Online* (10.1093/oxfordhb/9780199935413.013.61).

Robins, G. & C. Shute (1987). *The Rhind Mathematical Papyrus: An ancient Egyptian text*. British Museum Press, London.

Roccati, A. (2014). 'Dating Ptahhotep's Maxims (Note Letterarie VI).' *Orientalia* 3: 238–40.

Rösling, H. with O. Rösling & A.R. Rönnlund (2018). *Factfulness: Ten reasons why we're wrong about the world—and why things are better than you think*. Sceptre, London.

Ryholt, K. (2021). 'The Storage of Papyri in Ancient Egypt.' In E. Cancik-Kirschbaum, J. Kahl & E-J. Lee (eds). *Collect and Preserve: institutional contexts of epistemic knowledge in pre-modern societies*. Episteme in Bewegung: Beiträge zur einer transdisziplinären Wissengeschichte 9. Otto Harrassowitz, Wiesbaden: 23–64.

Schäfer, H. (1905). *Urkunden der älteren Äthiopenkönige*. J. C. Hinrichs, Leipzig.

Shaw, I.M.E. & E. Bloxam (eds). (2020). *The Oxford Handbook of Egyptology*. Oxford University Press, Oxford.

Smither, P.C. (1942). 'An Old Kingdom Letter Concerning the Crimes of Count Sabni.' *Journal of Egyptian Archaeology* 28: 16–19.

Spade, P.V. (2007). *Thoughts, Words and Things. An introduction to late mediaeval logic and semantic theory*. http://www.pvspade.com/Logic/docs/Thoughts, %20Words%20and%20Things1_2.pdf.

Stauder, A. (2016). 'Ptahhotep 82P.' In P. Collombert, D. Lefèvre, S. Polis & J. Winand (eds). *Aere perennius. Mélanges égyptologiques en l'honneur de Pascal Vernus*. Orientalia Lovaniensia Analecta 242. Peeters, Leuven, Paris & Bristol, CT: 779–810.

Tallet, P. (2017). *Les papyrus de la Mer Rouge, 1. Le 'Journal de Merer' (Papyrus Jarf A et B)*. Mémoires de l' Institut Français d'archéologie Orientale 136. Cairo.

Tallet, P. & M. Lehner (2022). *The Red Sea Scrolls: How ancient papyri reveal the secrets of the pyramids*. Thames & Hudson, London & New York.

Taterka, F. (2017). 'Were Ancient Egyptian Kings Literate?' *Studien zur altägyptischen Kultur* 46: 267–83.

Taylor, J. (2000). 'The Third Intermediate Period (1069–664 BC).' In I.M.E. Shaw (ed.). *The Oxford History of Ancient Egypt*. Oxford University Press, Oxford: 324–63.

Tobin, V.A. (2003). 'The Maxims of Ptahhotep'. In W.K. Simpson (ed.). *The Literature of Ancient Egypt: An anthology of stories, instructions, stelae, autobiographies, and poetry*. 3rd edn. Yale University Press, New Haven & London: 129–48.

Török, L. (1997). *The Kingdom of Kush: Handbook of the Napatan-Meroitic Civilization*. Handbuch der Orientalisk. Brill, Leiden, New York & Köln.

Verner, M. (2010). 'Several Considerations Concerning the Old Kingdom Royal Palace.' *Anthropologie (Brno)* 48/2: 91–96.

Waddell, W.G. (1940). *Manetho*. Harvard University Press, Cambridge, MA.

Warburton, D.A. (2009). 'Time and Space in Ancient Egypt: The importance of the creation of abstraction.' In R. Nyord & A. Kjølby (eds). *Being in Ancient Egypt: Thoughts on agency, materiality and cognition*. BAR International, Oxford: 83–95.

Wilkinson, T.A.H. (2000). *Royal Annals of Ancient Egypt: The Palermo Stone and its associated fragments*. Kegan Paul International, London & New York.

Wiseman, P.J. (1977). *Clues to Creation in Genesis*. Marshall, Morgan & Scott, London.

Wittgenstein, L. (1922). *Tractatus Logico-Philosophicus*. Kegan Paul, Trench, Trübner & Co., London.

Žába, Z. (1956). *Les maximes de Ptahhotep*. Éditions de l'Académie Tchécoslovaque des Sciences, Prague.

ILLUSTRATION CREDITS

Illustrations are listed first by page number and then by plate number.

INDEX

INDEX